# Earth's Incredible Habitats
# Ocean

Written by
**Annie Roth**

Illustrated by
**Sandra Neuditschko**

**Penguin Random House**

**Written by** Annie Roth
**Illustrated by** Sandra Neuditschko
**Senior Editor** Ben Morgan
**Lead Designer** Anna Pond
**Editors** Jolyon Goddard, Lizzie Munsey
**US Editor** Jill Hamilton
**US Senior Editor** Shannon Beatty
**Designers** Hannah Moore, Lucy Sims
**Senior Picture Researcher** Sakshi Saluja
**Jacket Designer** Bettina Myklebust Støvne
**Jacket Illustrator** Joe Stansbury
**Jacket Coordinator** Elin Woosnam
**Managing Editor** Rachel Fox
**Managing Art Editor** Owen Peyton Jones
**Production Editor** Dragana Puvacic
**Producer** Ben Radley
**Publisher** Andrew Macintyre
**Art Director** Mabel Chan
**Managing Director** Sarah Larter

**Consultant** Dr. Rebecca Green

First American Edition, 2024
Published in the United States by DK Publishing,
a division of Penguin Random House LLC
1745 Broadway, 20th Floor, New York, NY 10019
Copyright © 2024 Dorling Kindersley Limited
25 26 27 28 10 9 8 7 6 5 4 3 2
002–343434–March/2025

Published in Great Britain by Dorling Kindersley Limited

A catalog record for this book
is available from the Library of Congress.
ISBN 978-0-5939-5923-7

DK books are available at special discounts when
purchased in bulk for sales promotions, premiums,
fund-raising, or educational use.
For details, contact: DK Publishing Special Markets,
1745 Broadway, 20th Floor, New York, NY 10019
SpecialSales@dk.com

Printed and bound in China

www.dk.com

# Contents

# North Atlantic

Stretching between the balmy tropics and the icy
Arctic is the North Atlantic Ocean. This stormy sea
has a great diversity of habitats. Wildlife is
especially rich on the continental shelves – the
relatively shallow areas close to Europe and North
America. Here, the water is warmed by the Gulf
Stream, a current from the Gulf of Mexico.

# South Atlantic

The South Atlantic lies between South America and Africa – a vast blue realm with few islands. Most of the wildlife hugs the continental coasts, where huge shoals of fish find rich pickings in the plankton – the tiny floating organisms in the surface. These fish are food in turn for predators such as the Atlantic sailfish. It herds prey into tight balls before stunning them with violent flicks of its spear-shaped bill.

# Pacific Ocean

The largest and deepest ocean, the Pacific is greater in area than all the world's land combined. Its name means "peaceful" and comes from European sailors who found the wind so calm near the equator that their ships would get stuck for weeks. Straddling the equator, the central Pacific has a tropical climate and is peppered with islands fringed by coral reefs.

# Indian Ocean

To the south of India is the world's third-largest ocean, the Indian Ocean. Much of this ocean has a warm, tropical climate – ideal for the coral reefs and mangrove forests that flourish around its coastline and many islands. Here, a shoal of Maldive anemonefish are guarding the stinging sea anemone that provides them with shelter in a coral reef.

# Arctic Ocean

Earth's coldest ocean, the Arctic, sits over the North Pole. It is so cold here in winter that much of the ocean freezes over. This might sound like a disaster for wildlife, but it provides nesting sites for seals and allows polar bears to walk across the sea. Meanwhile, sea mammals such as whales and walruses thrive under the frozen surface, their bodies kept warm by thick layers of blubber.

# Southern Ocean

The Southern Ocean surrounds the continent of Antarctica, which sits on Earth's South Pole. This ocean is famous for its stormy seas, icebergs, and giant waves, which make it dangerous for ships. However, it is rich in wildlife, from penguins and leopard seals to blue whales. These aquatic animals thrive in the chilly water, which teems with fish, krill, and other small animals.

## Ocean or sea?

Different parts of the ocean have distinct names, just as different areas of land have names. For instance, the great expanse of ocean to the south of India is called the Indian Ocean. Seas are smaller areas that are usually partly enclosed by land, such as the Red Sea.

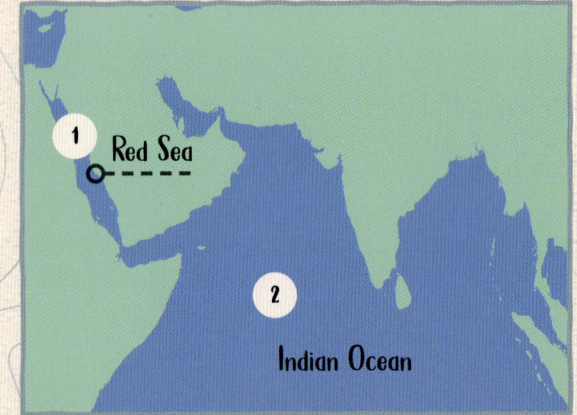

1 Red Sea

2 Indian Ocean

# What is an ocean?

A vast expanse of salty water covers 71 percent of Earth's surface. Although this is really a single ocean, we give names such as Atlantic and Pacific to different parts of it. We normally see only the surface of this watery world, but underneath is a hidden realm of mountains and canyons inhabited by strange forms of life. Even today, its deepest parts remain almost completely unexplored.

## The ocean floor

Just as there are mountains and valleys on land, there are landscapes on the seafloor. We see the tips of the tallest mountains as islands where they poke above the water, but there are many more hidden below.

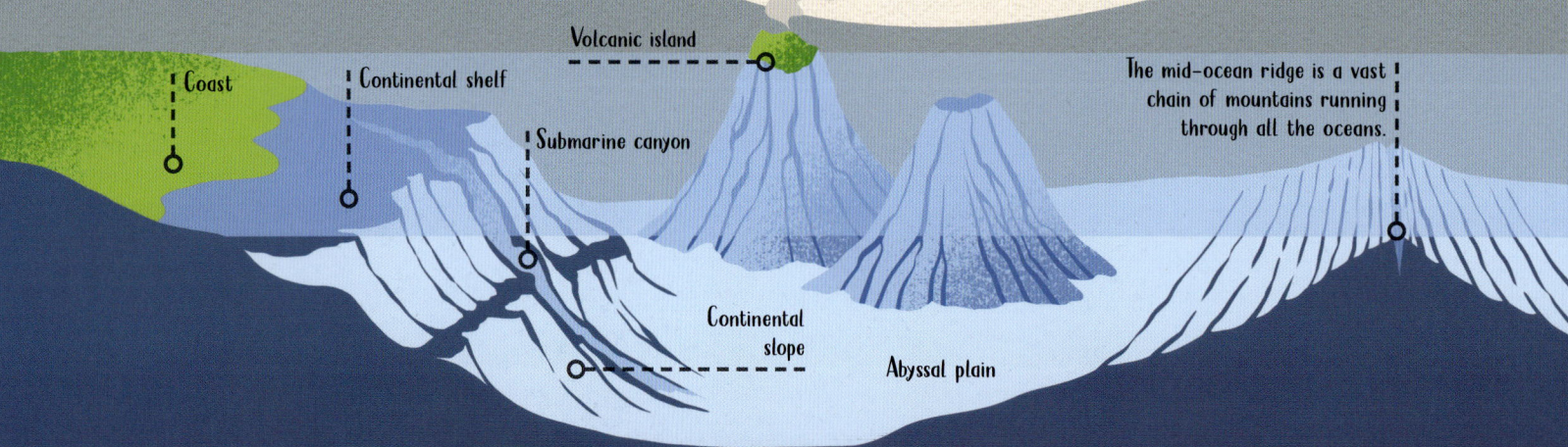

Coast

Continental shelf

Volcanic island

Submarine canyon

The mid-ocean ridge is a vast chain of mountains running through all the oceans.

Continental slope

Abyssal plain

# Ocean species

Life in the sea is quite different from life on land. With water to support their weight, animals can reach a great size, but they must be streamlined to move. To get oxygen, which is vital for life, sea creatures either need gills to extract it from water or they must rise to the surface to breathe and then hold their breath.

## Algae

There are few true plants in the sea. Instead, organisms called algae do the job of photosynthesis, creating food that animals eat. Seaweeds are algae that grow as big as plants, but most algae are microscopic.

## Crustaceans

Almost no insects live in the sea. Instead, crustaceans —such as crabs and shrimps—take their place. These small animals have jointed exoskeletons like insects but also gills for breathing in water.

## Animal or plant?

Some sea animals, such as this feather star, look like plants. These creatures feed by catching floating bits of food with feathery organs that work like nets.

## Mapping the seafloor

Scientists use sound to work out how deep the sea is: the longer it takes for an echo to return, the deeper the water. By doing this throughout the oceans, scientists can map the whole seafloor.

Sound waves bounce off the seafloor and return as echoes.

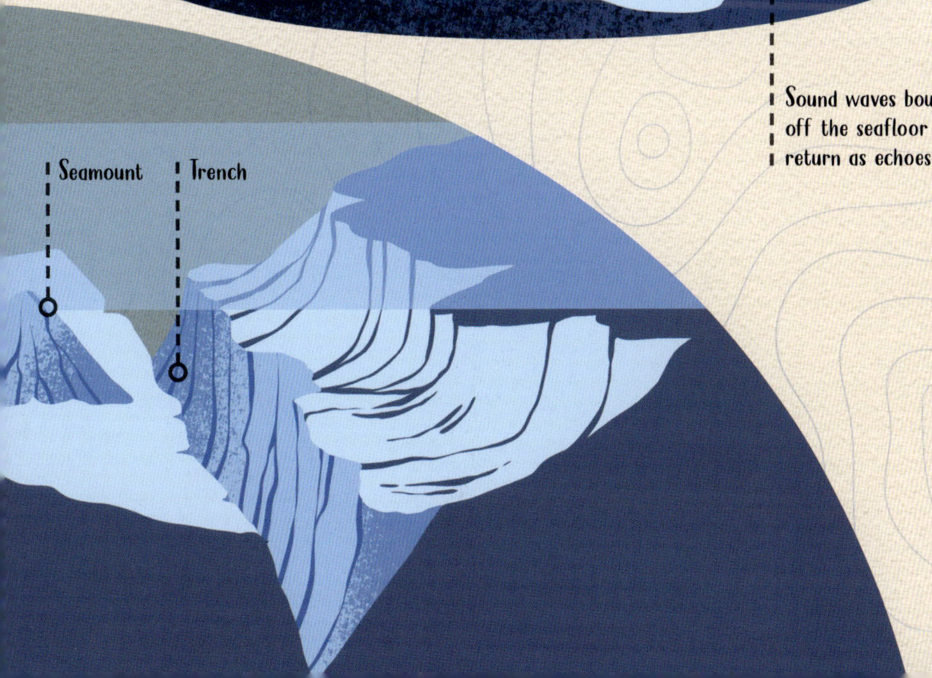

Seamount   Trench

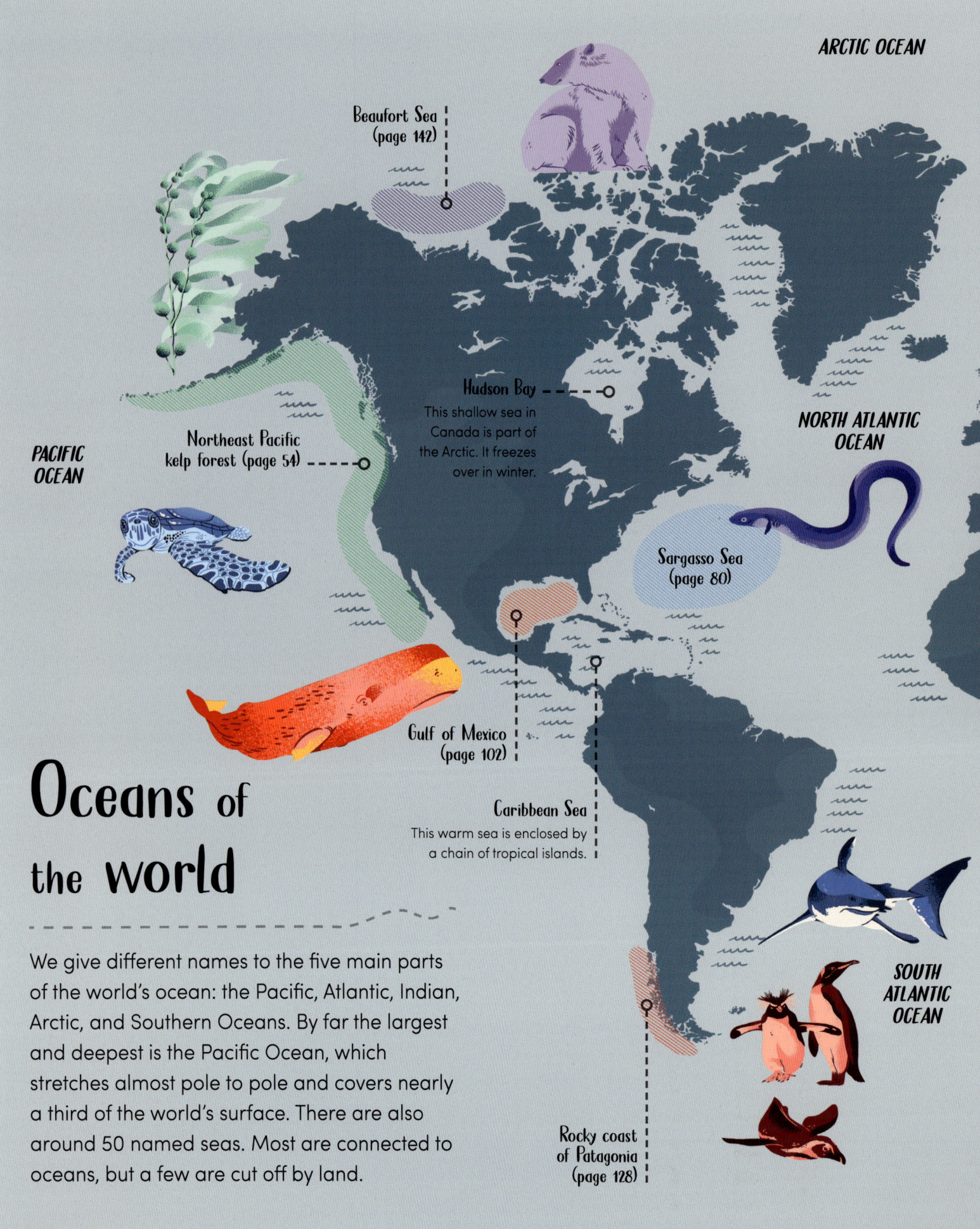

ARCTIC OCEAN

Beaufort Sea
(page 142)

Hudson Bay
This shallow sea in
Canada is part of
the Arctic. It freezes
over in winter.

NORTH ATLANTIC
OCEAN

PACIFIC
OCEAN

Northeast Pacific
kelp forest (page 54)

Sargasso Sea
(page 80)

Gulf of Mexico
(page 102)

Caribbean Sea
This warm sea is enclosed by
a chain of tropical islands.

SOUTH
ATLANTIC
OCEAN

Rocky coast
of Patagonia
(page 128)

# Oceans of the world

We give different names to the five main parts
of the world's ocean: the Pacific, Atlantic, Indian,
Arctic, and Southern Oceans. By far the largest
and deepest is the Pacific Ocean, which
stretches almost pole to pole and covers nearly
a third of the world's surface. There are also
around 50 named seas. Most are connected to
oceans, but a few are cut off by land.

**Baltic Sea**
The shallow Baltic Sea is enclosed by the countries of northern Europe.

**Black Sea**
This inland sea is connected to the Mediterrean Sea.

**Caspian Sea**
Sometimes called a lake, the Caspian Sea is the world's largest inland body of water. Its water is about a third as salty as seawater.

*PACIFIC OCEAN*

**Mediterranean Sea**
This warm sea is famous for its many beaches and islands.

*INDIAN OCEAN*

**Sundarbans mangrove forest (page 116)**

**Mariana Trench (page 92)**

**The Great Barrier Reef (page 28)**

**Shark Bay seagrass meadow (page 66)**

**Red Sea**
Between the deserts of Africa and Arabia is the Red Sea, a busy route for ships.

**Bora Bora atoll (page 40)**

*SOUTHERN OCEAN*

# Marine habitats

Just as there are forests, grasslands, and deserts on land, there are different kinds of habitat in the sea. Many sea creatures live in coastal habitats, where the sun is bright and the shallow seafloor provides places to hide or rocks to cling to. Other animals spend their lives far out at sea, either adrift in the current or on an endless swim. The toughest marine habitat of all is the deep sea, where there is very little to eat and it's perpetually dark and cold.

## Food chains

Nearly all the world's natural habitats are powered by the Sun's energy. Light energy is captured by organisms such as plants and used to make food. The energy in food then passes from one animal to another along a food chain. On land, plants form the base of food chains. In the ocean, tiny floating organisms called phytoplankton are the base of most food chains.

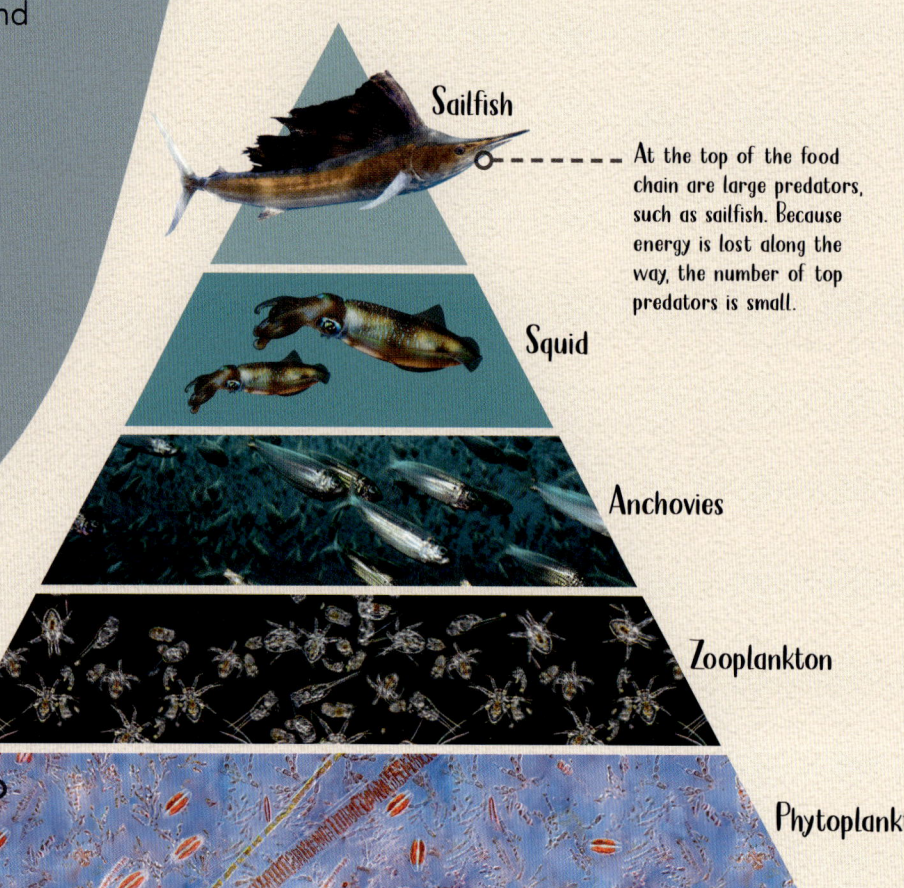

Sailfish

At the top of the food chain are large predators, such as sailfish. Because energy is lost along the way, the number of top predators is small.

Squid

Anchovies

Zooplankton

A single drop of seawater may contain thousands of phytoplankton.

Phytoplankton

## Depth zones

Far from land is the open ocean, where the water is very deep. Scientists divide the open ocean into habitats based on depth. As you go deeper, the water gets colder and darker. At the bottom of the deep sea, it's pitch black and as cold as the inside of a refrigerator.

SUNLIT ZONE

TWILIGHT ZONE

MIDNIGHT ZONE

ABYSSAL ZONE

HADAL ZONE

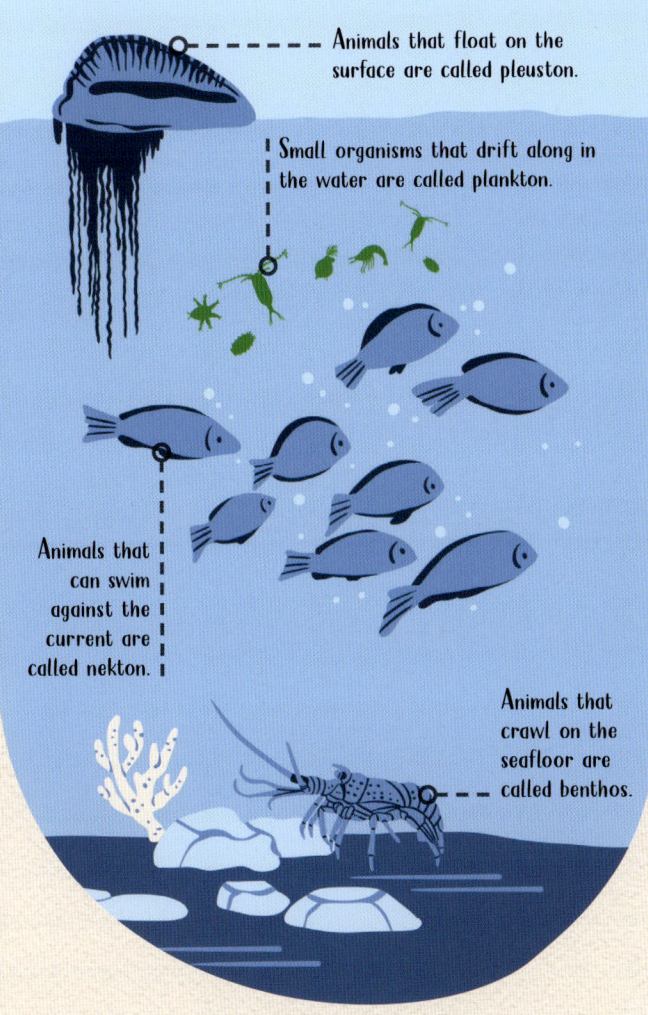

Animals that float on the surface are called pleuston.

Small organisms that drift along in the water are called plankton.

Animals that can swim against the current are called nekton.

Animals that crawl on the seafloor are called benthos.

## Sink or swim?

Scientists classify marine animals by the way they move in water. Some animals are so small they have no choice but to drift wherever the water carries them. These are called plankton. Others are big and strong enough to swim against the current or crawl along the bottom, and a few animals float on the surface like balloons.

# Coastal habitats

Most life in the sea is near the coast, where the water is shallow and sunlight can reach the seafloor. Whether rocky or sandy, the seabed provides habitats for many kinds of animal. Coastal waters are also rich in nutrients washed into the sea by rivers.

### Kelp forests

Most seaweeds are small and slimy, but kelp grows as tall as a tree and forms underwater forests. These green havens provide shelter and hunting grounds for sea otters, sea lions, and even some whales.

### Coral reefs

Near tropical coasts, the dead skeletons of tiny animals called corals pile up over centuries to create raised areas called reefs. Coral reefs have a greater diversity of marine life than any other ocean habitat.

### Seagrass meadows

Grassy meadows don't just grow on land—they also flourish in warm, shallow seas. Instead of cows and sheep, there are huge, grass-eating aquatic animals called sea cows.

### Rocky coasts

Nooks and crannies on rocky coasts provide holes for animals. When the tide goes out, animals survive in tide pools, bury themselves in sand, or simply close their shells and wait.

# Life in the deep

There's no light in the deepest parts of the ocean, but there's still life. Most of the strange animals that live here get energy from the "rain" of dead matter falling from high above. Some animals, like these mussels, get energy from hot volcanic springs on the seafloor.

## All the world's water

Our planet has a limited supply of water. The total volume of water in the oceans, glaciers, lakes, rivers, and so on is 0.3 billion cubic miles (1.4 billion cubic km). It might sound like a lot, but it's only 0.1 percent of Earth's volume.

Earth only has enough water to make a sphere 860 miles (1,380 km) wide.

# Water

The oceans contain about 97 percent of Earth's water, mostly in liquid form. Without liquid water, life on our planet would be impossible. Your body is about 60 percent water, and every other animal and plant is mostly water too. Fortunately for us, Earth is just the right temperature for water on the surface to be in its liquid state. On every other planet we know of, the water is frozen solid, a gas, or there's none at all.

## Waves

Waves are caused by wind blowing on the sea surface. Water doesn't actually travel in waves. Instead, waves transmit energy, which makes the water bob up and down as energy passes through it, just as a buoy or a boat bobs up and down. When a wave reaches the shore, the seafloor interferes with this motion and water piles up before tumbling over in a shower of white foam—a breaker.

The sun's warmth makes seawater evaporate. The water vapor forms clouds.

Clouds rise and cool as they cross land, causing rain and snow.

Rainwater returns to the ocean in rivers and underground.

# The water cycle

The water you drink is the same water that the dinosaurs drank. Earth's water moves between sea, sky, and land in a never-ending cycle. This cycle brings water to land, allowing life to flourish. After falling as rain and snow on land, water flows back to the sea, carrying salt and other nutrients that help marine life.

# Tides

Every day, the sea rises and falls. It floods beaches as it rises and then uncovers them as it goes back out again. These movements are called tides. They are caused by the moon, which pulls on the ocean with the force of gravity. At St. Michael's Mount in the UK, low tide reveals a hidden road that leads to the island—if you're quick enough!

High tide

Low tide

# Ocean currents

The water in the ocean isn't still. It flows around in huge streams called currents, driven by Earth's spin and by the wind. Some currents travel in giant circles around the ocean surface. Others snake slowly along the ocean floor—these deep currents take 1,000 years to travel around the world.

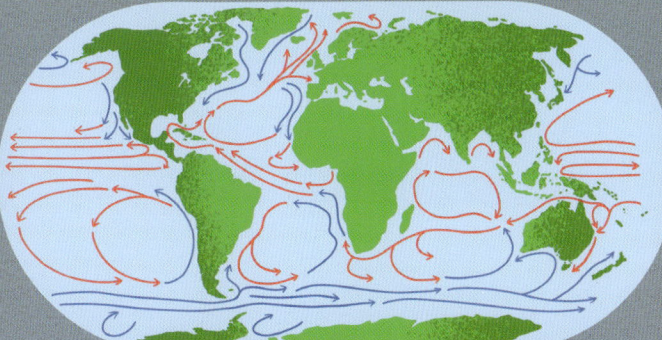

Warm currents

Cool currents

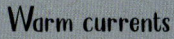

## Plastic garbage

Every year, more than 9 million tons of waste plastic ends up in the sea. Large plastic objects can trap or choke sea animals. Much of the plastic breaks down into tiny fragments—microplastics—but these are harmful too as they're eaten by filter-feeders (animals that filter food from the water).

Worms burrow in methane ice on the seafloor.

# Threats

Ocean habitats are essential to life on Earth. Most of the oxygen in the air we breathe comes not from plants on land but from tiny, plantlike organisms in the sea. Oceans also stabilize Earth's climate by absorbing carbon dioxide. However, many ocean habitats are under threat because of human activity.

## Methane burps

The seafloor contains vast reserves of the greenhouse gas methane in a solid form called methane ice. Some scientists think mass extinctions in the past were caused by "methane burps"—sudden release of methane from the sea, leading to catastrophic global warming. Fortunately, most scientists think another methane burp is unlikely to happen anytime soon.

## Warming oceans

Global warming doesn't just affect temperatures on land—it makes the sea warmer too. This is bad news for coral reefs as coral organisms lose the tiny, plantlike cells that live inside them when the water is too warm. This causes "coral bleaching"—the corals turn white and die.

# Acidic seas

Rising levels of $CO_2$ (carbon dioxide) in the atmosphere cause rising levels in the sea too. But $CO_2$ turns into carbonic acid when it dissolves in water. As a result, the oceans are becoming more acidic, harming sea life. This sea snail should have a perfectly clear shell, but acidification has made it cloudy and weak.

# Habitat loss

The richest marine habitats are near the coast, but people like living or spending vacations near the coast too. As coastal cities expand, natural habitats are replaced by roads, buildings, and ports. Pollution, sewage, and litter from these urban environments end up in the sea.

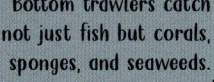

Bottom trawlers catch not just fish but corals, sponges, and seaweeds.

The heavy steel doors that keep trawler nets open scrape across the seafloor, damaging habitats.

# Overfishing

Overfishing happens when people catch fish faster than fish can breed. This causes fish populations to fall. Some fishing boats do even more damage by using a technique called bottom trawling. This involves dragging a net across the seafloor, which catches everything in its path and harms seafloor habitats.

# Oil spills

Oil spills occur when oil leaks out of tankers or offshore oil wells and spreads across the sea surface. Seabirds and marine mammals can get covered in the sticky oil, making it hard for them to fly, swim, or stay warm. Oil can also poison fish and other animals if it enters their gills or gets swallowed.

25

# Coral reefs

Coral reefs are sometimes called the rainforests of the ocean because they are so full of life. Despite covering less than 0.1 percent of the seafloor, they are home to more than 25 percent of all marine fish species. These colorful habitats are found in shallow tropical seas and are built by colonies of tiny animals called coral polyps. Coral reefs need clean water of just the right temperature to thrive, which makes them very sensitive to changes in their environment.

AUSTRALIA

## Visible from space

The Great Barrier Reef is sometimes described as the largest living structure on Earth. Apart from human cities, it is the only structure built by animals that is visible from space. That's an impressive achievement for coral organisms, which are only a fraction of an inch wide each.

The Great Barrier Reef lies in shallow water close to the shore.

AUSTRALIA

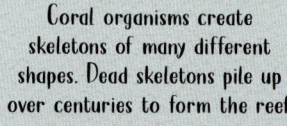

Coral organisms create skeletons of many different shapes. Dead skeletons pile up over centuries to form the reef.

## Coral colors

When seen up close, the Great Barrier Reef is a kaleidoscope of different colors. Corals use colored pigments as suncreens to protect themselves from sunlight. Fish and other animals use bright colors as warning signs, as signals to identify their species, and even as camouflage to hide in coral.

# The Great Barrier Reef

**Area**
133,000 square miles
(344,400 sq km)

**Length**
1,429 miles (2,300 km)

**Age**
Oldest parts are more
than 500,000 years old

FACT FILE

Australia's Great Barrier Reef is the largest coral reef system in the world.

The Great Barrier Reef consists of around 3,000 reefs and 1,000 islands off Australia's northeastern coast. Altogether, it covers 133,000 square miles (344,400 sq km), making it roughly the same size as Japan. This vast ecosystem is home to more than 9,000 species, some of which are found nowhere else. Most of the Great Barrier Reef is protected, so its animals are safe from things like overfishing and oil drilling. However, climate change poses a major threat to the Great Barrier Reef as rising sea surface temperatures are causing its corals to die off.

## Coral city

Coral reefs are the megacities of the underwater world. They have a greater density of species than any other ocean habitat.

The Great Barrier Reef is home to 133 species of sharks and rays.

# Geography of the Great Barrier Reef

The Great Barrier Reef is an ancient structure made by small, flower-shaped animals called coral polyps or simply corals. Most corals live in shallow tropical seas, where the water is warm and there's plenty of sunlight. Living corals grow atop the remains of their dead ancestors. Over time, their skeletons pile up on the seabed to form a raised structure—a reef. Reefs are full of nooks and crannies that provide homes and hiding places for countless other sea creatures.

## Structure of coral

Most corals grow in colonies of hundreds of thousands working together. Each individual is known as a polyp and is about the size of a lentil. There are two kinds of coral: hard and soft. Hard corals build hard skeletons made of the mineral limestone (calcium carbonate) for support and protection.

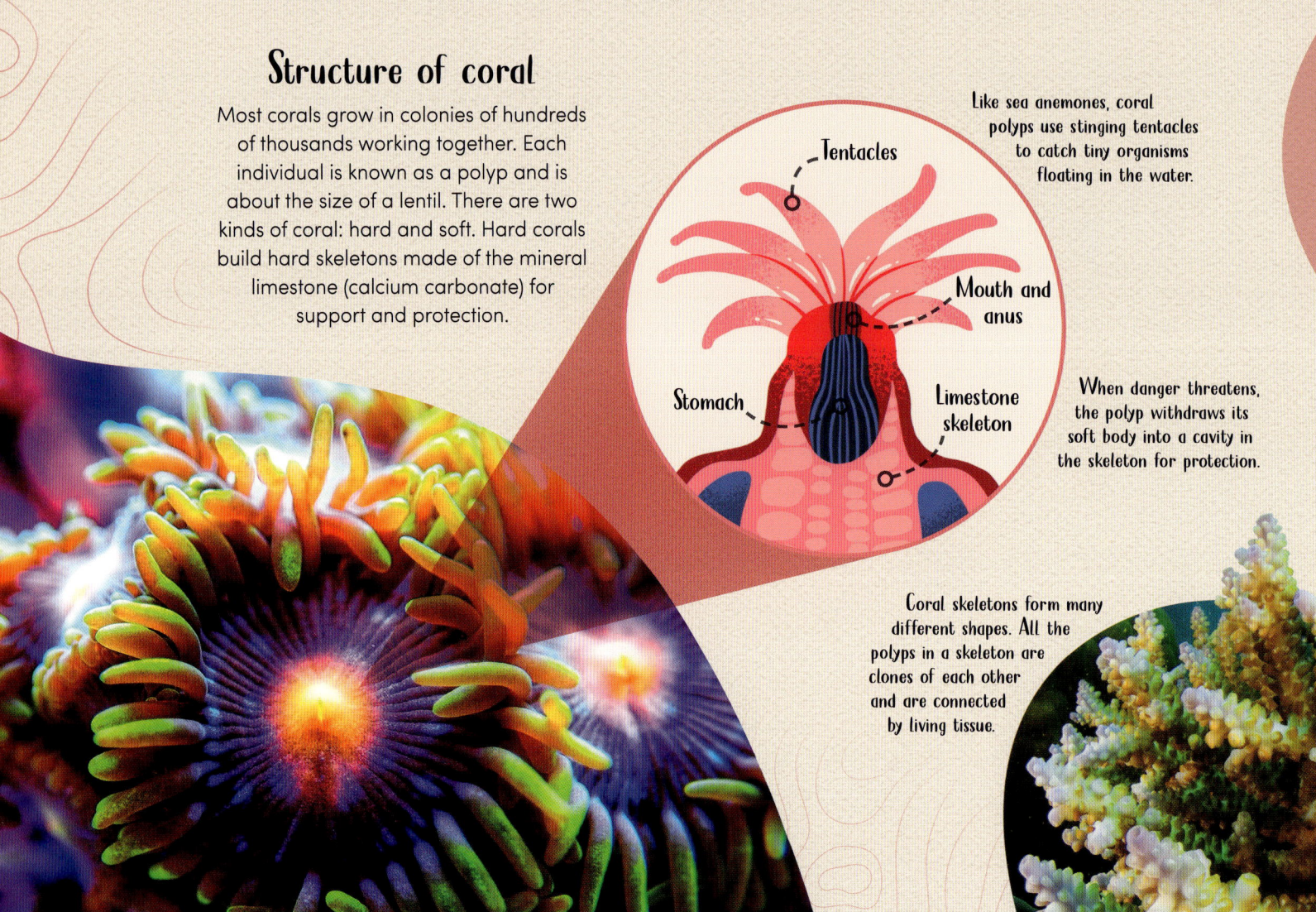

Like sea anemones, coral polyps use stinging tentacles to catch tiny organisms floating in the water.

Tentacles

Mouth and anus

Stomach

Limestone skeleton

When danger threatens, the polyp withdraws its soft body into a cavity in the skeleton for protection.

Coral skeletons form many different shapes. All the polyps in a skeleton are clones of each other and are connected by living tissue.

## Reefs and lagoons

The Great Barrier Reef is not a single reef but a diverse ecosystem made up of coral reefs, islands, lagoons, and mangrove forests. In this photo from a plane, the coral reef looks brown. The green and blue pools are shallow lagoons with floors of coral sand—tiny grains of dead coral skeleton.

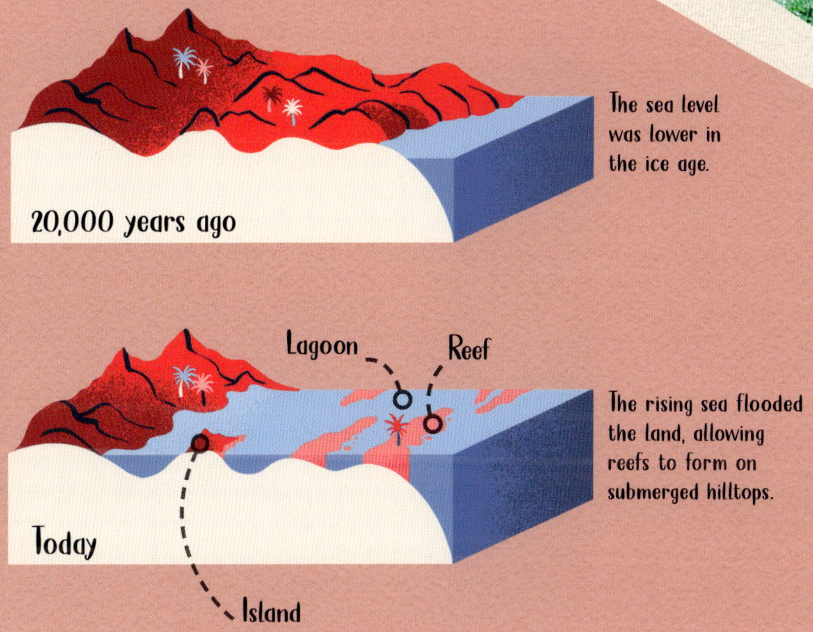

The sea level was lower in the ice age.

20,000 years ago

Lagoon     Reef

The rising sea flooded the land, allowing reefs to form on submerged hilltops.

Today

Island

## How it formed

The oldest parts of the Great Barrier Reef are more than half a million years old, but the current living structure began forming 20,000 years ago during the ice age. As the ice age faded, melting ice raised sea levels, flooding Australia's east coast. Corals thrived in the shallow, sunlit waters atop the region's flooded hills, forming reefs that have continued growing ever since.

## Food from light

Most corals need light because their polyps contain microscopic, plantlike organisms called zooxanthellae. These microbes use sunlight to make food by photosynthesis, helping coral grow. When corals get stressed by pollution or high temperatures, they lose their zooxanthellae, and the corals eventually die.

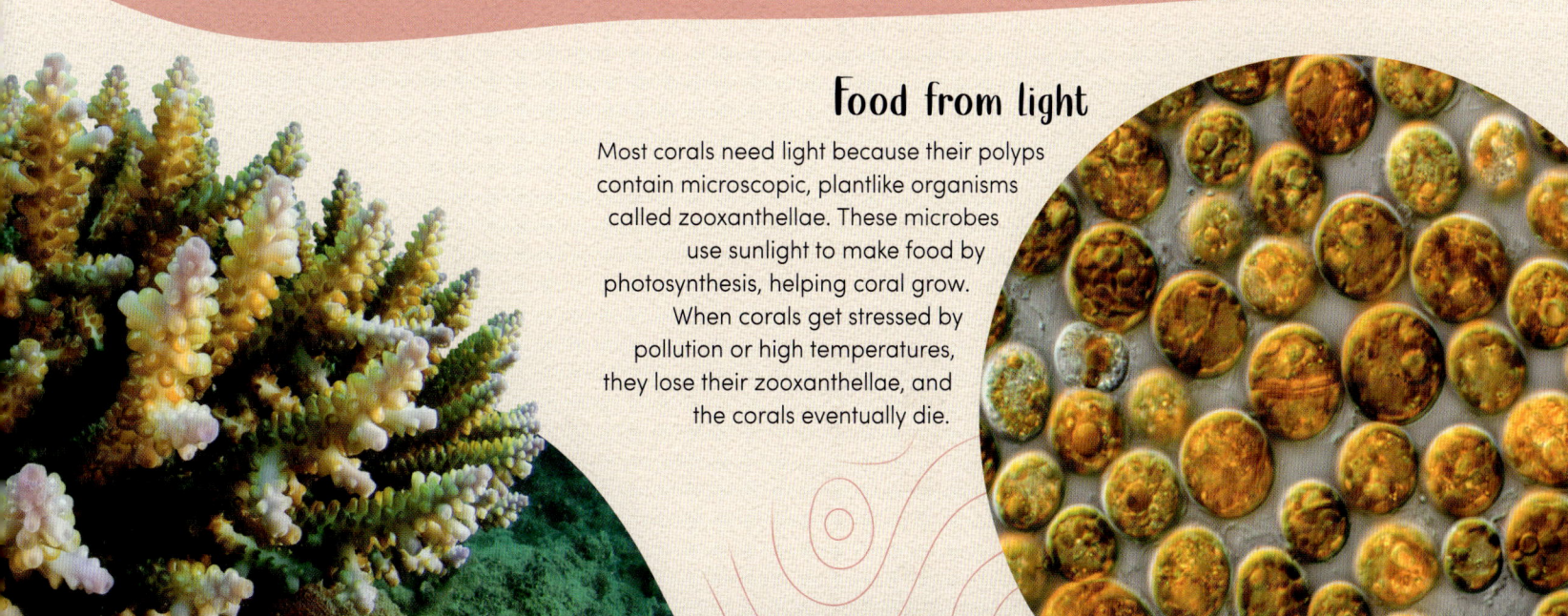

### Orange clownfish
#### (Amphiprion percula)

This little fish hides from danger among the stinging tentacles of sea anemones and is immune to the stings. It repays the favor by keeping anemones free of parasites and letting them eat its leftover food.

### Green sea turtle
#### (Chelonia mydas)

This endangered turtle is a strict herbivore, feeding only on seagrass and algae. The diet makes the flesh under its shell a greenish color, giving the species its name. Green sea turtles grow slowly, taking up to 50 years to reach adulthood.

# Animals of the Great Barrier Reef

The Great Barrier Reef is home to a vast number of different animals, including at least 3,000 mollusk species, 1,600 fish, 1,300 crustaceans, 1,400 corals, and 240 birds. All these animals depend on coral in one way or another. Some, like the crown-of-thorns starfish, eat corals, while others, like sea snakes, seek shelter among them.

### Crown-of-thorns starfish
#### (Acanthaster planci)

This 21-armed starfish feeds on coral. It can't bite coral as it has no teeth. Instead, its stomach is pushed out of its mouth and wrapped around the coral to digest the coral's soft tissue, turning it into a kind of soup the starfish can absorb.

### Giant clam
#### (Tridacna gigas)

The world's largest shellfish is the giant clam, which weighs up to 550 lb (250 kg). Its blue lips direct light onto microbes that live in its flesh. The microbes make food by photosynthesis, helping the clam grow. The lips also have thousands of tiny eyes—if they spot danger, the clam snaps shut.

## Ornate wobbegong
### (Orectolobus ornatus)

This shark gets its name from an Australian word for beard. Its speckled pattern and the growths around its chin help camouflage it while it lies on the reef waiting to ambush prey. People often step on wobbegongs by mistake. Their bites are painful so watch out!

## Olive sea snake
### (Aipysurus laevis)

This highly venomous sea snake is longer than a rattlesnake. It spends its life at sea, searching the reef's cracks and crevices for fish, shrimp, and crabs. Like all reptiles, the olive sea snake breathes air. After gulping air at the surface, it can hold its breath for two hours by storing it in a single lung that extends all the way along its body.

## Potato cod
### (Epinephelus tukula)

This large fish can reach 7 ft (2 m) long and is named for its potato-shaped spots. It is an ambush predator, lurking in coral until prey is close enough to suck into its huge mouth. Like other fish in the grouper family, the potato cod can change sex from female to male as it ages.

## Master of disguise

Cuttlefish can change the color, pattern, texture, and shape of their skin for perfect camouflage. This magical ability makes them almost invisible as they sneak up on prey. When spotted, they sometimes dazzle prey by changing repeatedly, making the victim easy to catch.

Camouflaged as coral

Camouflaged as rock

33

# Māori wrasse

One of the Great Barrier Reef's largest and most colorful fish is the Māori wrasse. Also known as the humphead wrasse thanks to its bulging forehead, this whopper can reach 7 ft (2 m) long and 420 lb (190 kg) in weight. It has a dynamic life cycle, able to change from female to male as it ages.

## Diver's friend

Māori wrasse are curious and bold creatures. They often swim close to scuba divers and can learn to recognize them, becoming more friendly over time.

## Life cycle

The Māori wrasse takes about five years to reach adulthood and can live for up to 30 years. Around nine years old, some females transition to "super-males," which are larger than other males and have bolder colors. Fish born male stay male all their life. The ability to change sex gives fish born female more opportunities to pass on their genes.

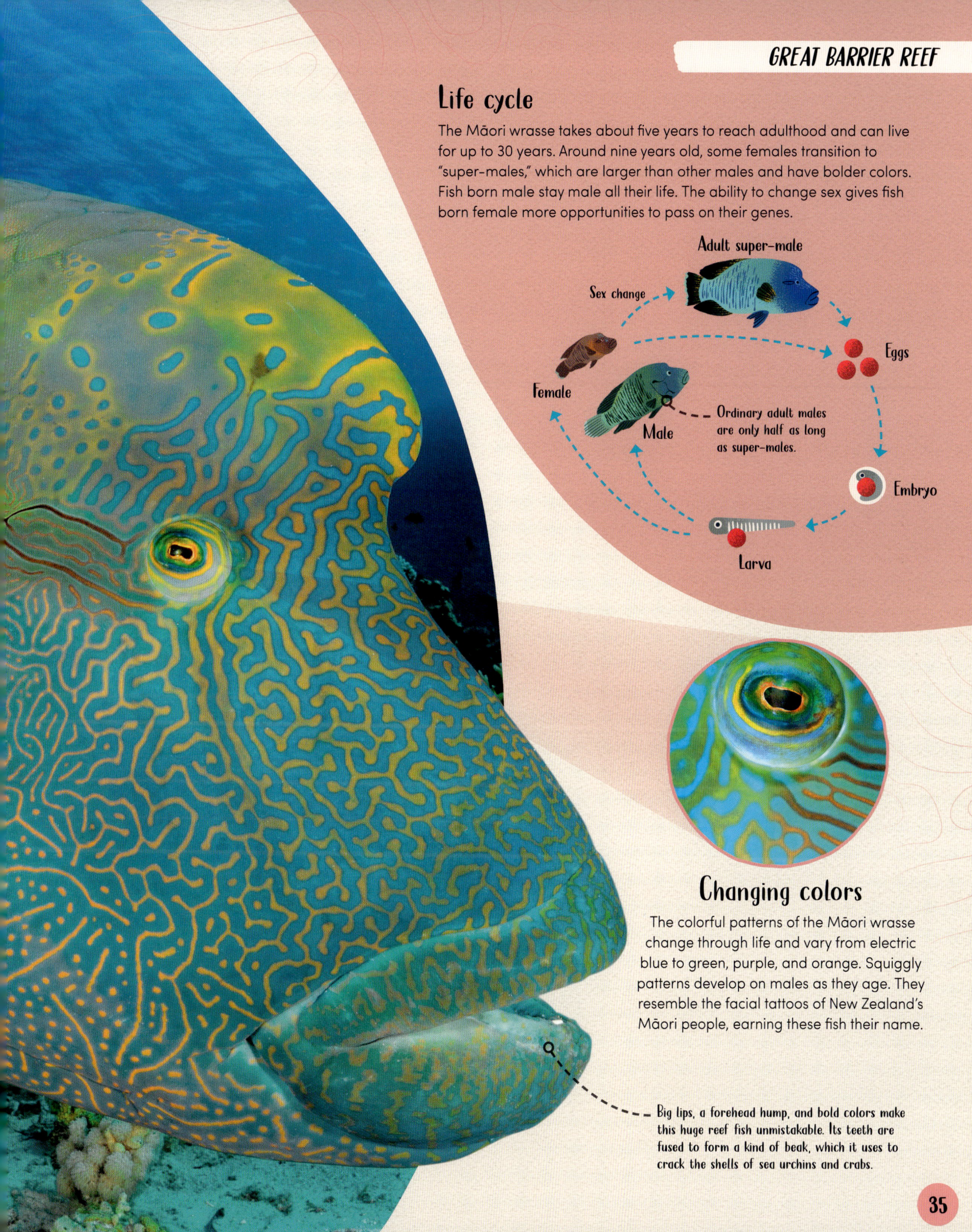

Adult super-male

Sex change

Female

Male

Ordinary adult males
are only half as long
as super-males.

Eggs

Embryo

Larva

## Changing colors

The colorful patterns of the Māori wrasse change through life and vary from electric blue to green, purple, and orange. Squiggly patterns develop on males as they age. They resemble the facial tattoos of New Zealand's Māori people, earning these fish their name.

Big lips, a forehead hump, and bold colors make this huge reef fish unmistakable. Its teeth are fused to form a kind of beak, which it uses to crack the shells of sea urchins and crabs.

## Filter feeder

The giant manta's diet consists largely of zooplankton, like these tiny copepods, but it also swims through schools of small fish and swallows huge numbers in one gulp.

# Giant manta ray

With a 23 ft (7 m) wingspan—about as wide as a light aircraft—the giant manta ray is among the largest fish in the ocean. It glides gracefully through the water, slowly flapping its huge pectoral fins, and feeds by filtering small animals from the water using a kind of sieve between its mouth and gills.

## Hitchhikers

Remoras (suckerfish) love hitching rides on manta rays. They stick to the ray using a special dorsal fin that acts like a suction cup, only letting go to suck up scraps from the ray's meals.

## Cleaning station

All along the Great Barrier Reef are places known as cleaning stations, which large marine animals visit to get clean. Small reef fish nibble away the visitor's dead skin and any parasites they find—free of charge!

# Heart Reef

In many parts of the Great Barrier Reef, corals have built up to form ring shapes around low areas on the seafloor. One of the most famous is Heart Reef, a 55-foot (17 m)-wide reef that has naturally formed in the shape of a heart. Coral reefs continually change shape, growing upward and outward by a few inches a year, but they cannot grow above the surface of the water.

**Area**
15.4 square miles
(40 sq km)

**Age**
7 million years

**Tallest points**
Mount Otemanu
2,385 ft (727 m)

# Bora Bora atoll

## This volcanic island in the heart of the Pacific Ocean is surrounded by a ring of coral reef—an atoll.

Atolls form in the shallow waters around tropical islands. Over time, the central island may erode away and disappear, but the coral reef remains, enclosing a lagoon of crystal-clear water that is bursting with life. Bora Bora still has its central island—the remains of an ancient volcano that is now extinct.

### Shelter belt

The outer reef around an atoll shelters the inner lagoon from waves and coastal currents. This creates a safe haven for all sorts of different sea creatures.

## Coral islands

Bora Bora's main island is mountainous, but it is surrounded by small coral islands that sit just above sea level. These islands may disappear if sea levels continue to rise due to global warming.

## Coral gardens

Bora Bora is home to several coral gardens—areas where colorful corals of several species grow together. One of the most famous coral gardens in Bora Bora is known as "the aquarium."

Lagoon

Mount
Otemanu

Coral reef

## Sinking island

Bora Bora's central island is slowly sinking into the sea, at a rate of a couple of inches a year. The reef surrounding it is the remains of a volcanic crater, which formed when the volcano that was once here blew itself apart.

## Blue waters

Separated from the open ocean, the lagoons that surround Bora Bora's main island are shallow and quiet. Their waters appear blue-green because they are so shallow and because of the way sunlight reflects off the trillions of tiny pieces of crushed-up corals in the lagoon.

# Geography of Bora Bora

Bora Bora is all that remains of a volcano that went cold millions of years ago. The ring-shaped reef that surrounds it is mostly underwater, but some parts have become smothered in sand, forming low-lying islands. Enclosed within this ring is a beautiful turquoise lagoon, whose sandy floor is peppered with coral. On the outside of the reef is a wall of coral, which faces the ocean.

## How atolls form

Atolls begin to form when an undersea volcano erupts, creating a new island. A coral reef forms around the new island. Then, once the volcano runs out of lava, it starts to sink. Eventually it disappears, leaving behind a ring of coral.

An erupting volcano forms a new island. Over time, coral reefs grow around it.

Later, the volcano stops being active and starts to sink back down under the water.

## Tropical temperatures

The temperature in Bora Bora is a balmy 26°C (80°F) or higher all year round. This is because Bora Bora sits close to Earth's equator. Its tropical waters are ideal for coral growth.

The area around the equator receives more direct sunlight than anywhere else on the planet.

• Bora Bora

The disappearing island leaves behind a lagoon, surrounded by coral reefs.

## Coral sand

Much of the beautiful white sand in Bora Bora is made of crushed-up coral skeletons. Dead corals erode into sand naturally, but parrotfish speed up this process by eating coral and pooping out sand. Scientists estimate that large adult parrotfish poop out over a ton of sand every year.

43

## Moray eel
### (Muraenidae)

These top predators of the reef have two sets of jaws and teeth: one set in the mouth and another in the throat. They latch on to prey with the teeth in their mouth, then the jaws in their throat extend outward, grab the prey, and pull it in.

## Hawksbill turtle
### (Eretmochelys imbricata)

Hawksbill turtles are named for their birdlike beaks, which they use to pull sponges from crevices in the reef. They are the only species of sea turtle whose diet consists mainly of sponges and whose shell has a jagged edge. Adult hawksbills are about 3 ft (1 m) long and weigh up to 180 lb (80 kg).

# Animals of Bora Bora

Few large animals live on Bora Bora's volcanic island, but its waters are overflowing with them. The coral reefs and lagoons are home to fish, sea turtles, sharks, rays, dolphins, and octopuses. Many of the species found here are also found in coral reefs in other parts of the world too.

## Unicorn fish
### (Naso unicornis)

These seaweed-eating reef dwellers have a hornlike structure on their heads, which may be used to attract mates. Males and females both have horns, and males can change the color of their horns to make themselves stand out during the breeding season.

## Trumpetfish
### (Aulostomus chinensis)

Trumpetfish sneak up on prey by hiding behind bigger, non-predatory fish. They can also change color to blend in with their surroundings or disguise themselves as objects such as sticks and seaweed.

## Stonefish
### (Synanceia verrucosa)

The stonefish is the most venomous fish on Earth. It has 13 sharp dorsal (back) spines, which secrete a powerful venom that can cause heart failure, paralysis, and even death. Stonefish are also masters of camouflage, which makes them easy to step on accidentally.

## White-tailed tropicbird
### (Phaethon lepturus)

These sea-faring birds spend nearly their entire lives over the open ocean, only coming to land to nest. They have a pair of tail feathers that are 16 in (40 cm) long and act as stabilizers during difficult aerial maneuvers.

## Day octopus
### (Octopus cyanea)

Most octopuses hunt at night, but the day octopus hunts when the sun is still shining. Its incredible ability to change the color and texture of its skin helps it sneak up on prey without being seen.

## Sea fan
### (Gorgonia)

There are more than 500 species of sea fans, and several of them can be found in Bora Bora. Their soft skeletons grow in a flat, branching pattern that makes a fan shape about 2 ft (60 cm) long.

## Sharing skeletons

A coral structure isn't a single living thing. It is the shared skeleton of hundreds of small animals called coral polyps. Each polyp has a ring of stinging tentacles to catch plankton.

## Mushroom coral
### (Fungiidae)

These unusual corals don't cement themselves to a surface; they can move around. Each mushroom coral consists of one large polyp, unlike most other corals, which are formed of groups of polyps.

# Corals of Bora Bora

Bora Bora is home to dozens of species of corals, each more dazzling than the last. They come in all shapes and sizes, from beanbags and brains to cauliflowers and mushrooms, with colors ranging from bubblegum pink to bright blue. Some of them are soft, while others form hard, stony outer skeletons.

## Table coral
### (Acropora)

This stony coral grows horizontally to form a flat shape like a table, giving its polyps better access to sunlight. Table corals grow much faster than other corals and can help to regenerate damaged coral reef habitats.

## Bubble coral
### (Plerogyra)

Bubble coral, also known as grape coral, has large, fleshy polyps that fill with water during the day. At night, the polyps deflate and the coral's tentacles emerge to feed on plankton.

## Cauliflower coral
### (Pocillopora)

The skeleton of this coral looks a bit like a cauliflower. It is tougher than most corals and can withstand powerful waves. The polyps in cauliflower coral are hermaphrodites, which means that each one is male as well as female.

## Elegance coral
### (Catalaphyllia)

This green-and-pink-striped coral is as elegant as its name suggests. Because of its vivid colors, it has been overharvested in the wild for use in aquariums and is now endangered. It can be found living in a colony or as a lone polyp.

# Great hammerhead

The great hammerhead is one of the biggest sharks in Bora Bora and the largest of the hammerhead sharks. Like all hammerhead sharks it has a very wide and flat head, with eyes on either end. This strange shape improves both the shark's 3D vision and a special electrical sense that it uses to find its prey. Young hammerheads are at risk of being eaten, but as adults the only predators they have to worry about are orcas.

Sphyrna mokarran

## Sleek swimmer

The great hammerhead is a powerful swimmer, capable of reaching 25 mph (40 kph), which is as quick as an Olympic sprinter. Its head is not only wide but flat too, which helps it move smoothly through the water.

## Scaly skin

The skin of the great hammerhead, like that of most sharks, is covered in thousands of hard, prickly scales that all point backward. These scales make water flow past smoothly, helping the shark swim faster and with less effort. The electron microscope image here shows the scales magnified to 100 times their actual size.

## Hammer scanner

Sharks use special receptors in their heads to detect electrical fields around prey. The hammerhead's long head has so many receptors that it can even detect stingrays and other animals hidden beneath the sand.

Receptors in the head detect changes in electrical energy in the water, which are created by moving prey.

## Regrowing teeth

Like other sharks, hammerheads keep growing new teeth throughout their lives. When a tooth falls out, a new one behind it moves forward to take its place.

# Humpback season

Between July and November, the sea around Bora Bora island is a sanctuary for humpback whales, which migrate to warm, tropical waters from the Antarctic to give birth and nurse their young. The babies weigh about 1.5 tons at birth and stay close to their mothers for 6–12 months.

# Forests and meadows

Most life on Earth on depends on the energy of the Sun, which is captured by photosynthesis and turned into food energy. On land, plants do this job, but in the oceans simpler organisms called algae do it instead. Most are microscopic, but in some places they grow as large as trees. Only a small number of true plants live in the sea, including seagrasses, which form green meadows in shallow, sunny waters.

**Length**
About 37,000 miles (60,000 km)

**Age**
At least 32 million years

**Dominant species**
Giant kelp
(*Macrocystis pyrifera*)

# Northeast Pacific kelp forest

Swaying majestically beneath the waves along the Pacific coast of North America are towering forests of kelp.

The kelp forest ecosystem is quite different from a forest on land. There are no plants here—only large, fast-growing seaweeds known as kelp. Some species, such as giant kelp, grow taller than most trees. Stretching from the dark seafloor to the sunlit surface, kelp forests provide a three-dimensional habitat to hundreds of different species, from urchins and otters to gray whales, the kelp forest's biggest visitor. Kelp forests cover about 580,000 square miles (1.5 million sq km) worldwide—an area five times greater than tropical coral reefs.

## Ocean acrobats

They may be clumsy and slow on land, but sea lions are graceful and agile underwater. They zip through the swaying kelp with ease, twisting and turning as they hunt fish, squid, and other prey.

Anchorage

In Alaska, wild kelp is harvested and turned into chips, pickles, and many other products.

Vancouver

## Around the world

Kelps are found off the coast of every continent except Antarctica. They thrive in cold, nutrient-rich waters where sunlight is plentiful.

GIANT KELP CAN GROW TEN TIMES TALLER THAN A GIRAFFE.

San Francisco

Los Angeles

## Channel Islands Marine Sanctuary

One-third of California's kelp forest is found around a group of small islands off the coast of Los Angeles. Sea otters were once common here, but they were hunted to extinction by the year 1900. The area is now a national marine sancutary.

Mexico City

# Geography of the Pacific kelp forest

Kelp forests grow along rocky coastlines in cooler parts of the world. The rocky seafloor provides anchorage for kelp, and the shallow coastal water ensures that kelp can reach the light. As well as providing food and habitats for all sorts of sea life, kelp forests protect the coast from erosion by waves. They also absorb carbon dioxide in the seawater, helping to combat climate change.

## Pounded by waves

The rocky coasts where kelp thrives are affected by crashing waves and changing tides. Kelp is well adapted to this harsh environment, with flexible stalks that can bend and stretch as they sway in the sea. Bull kelp can stretch to 40 percent longer before breaking. When the tide falls and kelp is exposed to the air, a gel-like substance called alginic acid stops it from drying out.

In winter, broken fragments of kelp wash up on the beaches of western Canada.

## Seasons in the sea

Like forests on land, kelp forests change with the seasons. In winter, stormy seas tear up the kelp, thinning the forest. But in spring it grows back, fueled by the ample sunlight streaming through gaps in the canopy. By fall the forest is restored and ready to endure another seasonal cycle.

## The fight for light

Kelps need light to survive as they make all their food by photosynthesis. The light is strongest at the surface, so kelps grow tall and many have gas-filled bladders to keep them buoyant. The competition for light is fierce—the winners not only bask in the sun but shade out potential rivals on the dark seafloor.

## Rocky seafloor

Different kinds of kelp grow in different places on a rocky coastline. The tallest types, such as giant kelp, do best in deep water. Nearer the shore, where the kelp has to withstand wave action and changing tides, tougher species like bull kelp and feather boa kelp thrive.

Giant kelp

Bull kelp

Featherboa kelp

Holdfasts anchor kelps to rocks

57

### Californian sea lion
*(Zalophus californianus)*

Often seen lounging on the shore, these marine mammals are icons of California, US. They are the fastest swimmers of all seals and sea lions, capable of reaching 25 mph (40 kph) in short bursts. Their color vision is limited to greens and blues, but this is perfect for hunting fish in a kelp forest.

# Animals of the Pacific kelp forest

Few ecosystems have a greater variety or density of animals than kelp forest. More than 1,000 species depend on this habitat for food, shelter, and safety. They include predators such as sea lions, which use kelp forests as safe havens in storms, and kelp-devouring urchins, which wreak havoc when their numbers rise.

### Sunflower sea star
*(Pycnopodia helianthoides)*

Measuring up to 3 ft (1 m) across and sporting a whopping 24 arms, the sunflower sea star is the world's largest starfish. These seafloor dwellers prey on sea urchins, sea cucumbers, snails, and smaller starfish.

## Swell shark
### (Cephaloscyllium ventriosum)

This harmless, ten-foot-long shark hides from predators by blending into the rocky seafloor. When that fails, it gulps seawater until its body balloons to double the size, making it difficult for a predator to swallow.

## Wolf eel
### (Anarrhichthys ocellatus)

Almost as long as an alligator and armed with a mouthful of crab-crushing teeth, the wolf eel is a fearsome predator. It hunts by hiding in a crevice and waiting to ambush victims that wander by. Wolf eels are born orange but turn gray with age for camouflage. They mate for life and parents cooperate to guard their eggs.

## Abalone
### (Haliotis)

Abalone are giant snails prized for their beautiful shells. The inside of the oval shell is lined with a rainbow-colored mineral called mother-of-pearl, which is used for making jewelry and ornaments. After being hunted to near extinction, abalone are now protected.

## Purple sea urchin
### (Strongylocentrotus purpuratus)

These spiky relatives of starfish love eating kelp. Predators like sea otters and sunflower sea stars protect kelp forest by keeping urchin numbers in check, but if the predator population falls, urchins explode in number and great swathes of kelp forest are destroyed.

## Inside a sea urchin

Between the defensive spines of a sea urchin are thousands of water-filled tube feet, which the animal uses to creep about on kelps or rocks. Sea urchins have no eyes but can see with their feet, which are sensitive to light. They also breathe with their feet, which absorb more oxygen from the water than their gills do.

Urchins have thousands of tube feet. Seawater is pumped into the feet to make them extend and move.

A brittle test (shell) with sharp spines protects the urchin from predators.

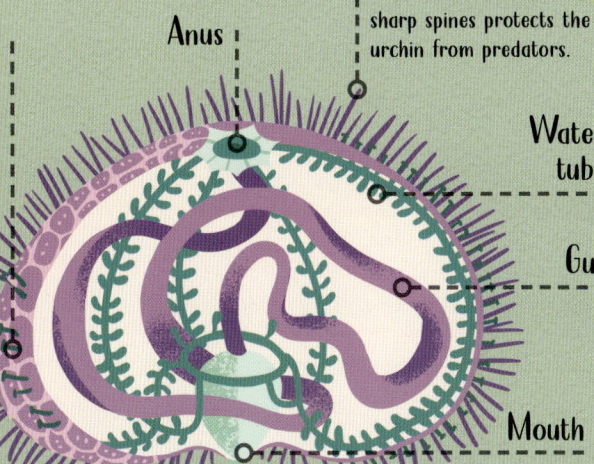

Anus

Water tube

Gut

Mouth

# Sea otter

This cute and charismatic mammal is found on coasts around the northern Pacific. It is better adapted to living in water than other otters and can spend its entire life in the sea. Although the sea otter is the only marine mammal without a thick layer of blubber, it can stay warm in the chilliest of waters thanks to its impressive fur coat.

## Bedtime

Unlike river otters, which sleep on land in underground dens, sea otters sleep floating in the sea. To prevent themselves from drifting away, they wrap themselves in kelp or hold hands with one another, forming groups called rafts.

## Tool users

Sea otters are among the few animals that use tools. They use rocks to crack open clams, crabs, and other hard-shelled prey. Sea otters often store their favorite rocks in a baggy pocket of loose skin beneath their forearms.

## Keystone species

In their kelp forest homes, sea otters are a keystone species, which means they help hold the ecosystem together. The otters eat sea urchins and other animals that feed on kelp. If otters weren't around, these grazers would consume every last speck of seaweed, turning a once thriving kelp forest into a lifeless landscape known as an "urchin barren."

## Fur coat

The sea otter has the densest fur of any animal, with around 1 million per square inch (155,000 hairs per sq cm). The super-dense and spiky hair traps a layer of air over the skin, keeping the otter warm in cold water. However, the air also increases buoyancy, limiting how deep sea otters can dive.

## Giant kelp
### (Macrocystis pyrifera)

Capable of reaching 174 ft (53 m) tall, giant kelp is the world's largest seaweed species. It also grows quickly, gaining up to 2 ft (60 cm) in height a day in ideal growing conditions. It has a short lifespan for such a large organism, typically living for only about seven years.

# Plants of the Pacific kelp forest

Strictly speaking, kelps are not plants but rather members of a class of organisms known to science as brown algae. Like plants, however, kelps photosynthesize, which means they capture the energy in sunlight and use it to make food molecules, supporting the rest of the kelp forest ecosystem. There are at least 30 different kinds of kelp, but the Pacific kelp forest is dominated by just two: giant kelp and bull kelp.

## Feather boa kelp
### (Egregia menziesii)

This dark brown kelp, found all the way from Alaska to Baja California, has many small blades that give it a feathery appearance. It grows to 16 ft (5 m) long and flourishes in the intertidal zone along rocky beaches.

## Bull kelp
### (Nereocystis luetkeana)

This sturdy kelp thrives in rough waters where waves are constantly crashing. Unlike giant kelp, which has blades all the way up its stipe, bull kelp has a tassel of blades at the top on a large gas bladder. This seaweed is safe to eat and tastes great when pickled.

## Elk kelp

*(Pelagophycus porra)*

Named for its antlerlike branches, elk kelp is one of the largest seaweeds in the kelp forest. Its super-long stipe, which can reach 98 ft (30 m), allows it to grow in deep water where other kelp species couldn't survive.

## Oarweed

*(Laminaria digitata)*

This small kelp grows to about 7 ft (2 m) long and so only thrives in shallow water close to the shore. This means the smooth, shiny blades are revealed at low tide when the sea retreats. Each blade is split into segments, like fingers on a hand.

## Stalked kelp

*(Pterygophora californica)*

Also known as woody-stemmed kelp, walking kelp, or winged kelp, stalked kelp has a tough, woody stipe that even has annual growth rings like a tree trunk. Most seaweeds live for only a few years, but stalked kelp is tough enough to survive for 25 years. Other seaweeds sometimes attach themselves to it to get closer to the light.

## Kelp anatomy

Kelps don't have roots as they can absorb water and nutrients from seawater. However, they have a rootlike structure called a holdfast to anchor themselves to the seafloor. Unlike plants on land, they hold themselves up with air-filled floats rather than sturdy stems.

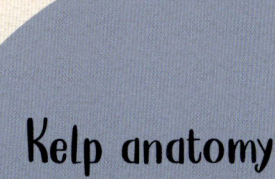

Air bladders make kelp float.

The soft, flexible stalk is called a stipe.

The parts that look like leaves are called blades.

A holdfast anchors the kelp to rock.

63

# Kelp refuge

California sea lions are agile swimmers but in open water they are no match for great white sharks, which often attack from below at speed. In a kelp forest, however, the sea lion's smaller size and greater agility give it an advantage. When danger threatens, it darts into the dense vegetation and vanishes from sight.

## Seagrass

Seagrasses are flowering plants, not seaweeds. Their pollen is carried from flower to flower by water and tiny marine crustaceans.

Australia

Australia

## Living fossils

Near Shark Bay's seagrass meadows are strange mounds of rock called stromatolites. Sometimes referred to as living fossils, these living structures are formed by the oldest forms of life on Earth—microscopic cells known as cyanobacteria.

**Shark Bay area**
8,500 square miles
(22,000 sq km)

**Seagrass meadow area**
1,550 square miles
(4,000 sq km)

**Seagrass species**
12

FACT FILE

# Shark Bay
# seagrass meadow

Located at Australia's most westerly point, Shark Bay is unlike any other place on Earth.

This sheltered bay is home to the world's largest expanse of seagrass, an aquatic plant that forms lush green meadows on the seafloor. Many large sea creatures live in or visit this underwater grassland, including dugongs, dolphins, turtles, and at least 28 species of sharks.

### Dugong

Also called sea cows, dugongs are distantly related to elephants but spend their whole lives in water. These slow-moving herbivores must eat around 66 lbs (30 kg) of seagrass a day to maintain their bulky bodies.

# Geography of Shark Bay

This shallow bay is a magical place where land and sea meet and mingle. Seawater flows into the bay as the tide rises and flows out again as it falls. The continual tidal changes move the sand around, creating pools, channels, and sandy beaches between strips of land colored rust red by Australia's soil.

## Where seagrass grows

Seagrass grows in sand or mud in shallow coastal areas where plenty of sunshine reaches the seafloor. It grows best where the water is clear and bright rather than dark and murky. Seagrass needs sunshine because it makes food by capturing the energy in sunlight (photosynthesis).

## Useless Loop

To the west of Shark Bay is the town of Useless Loop. It is far from useless: the site is used to manufacture salt from seawater. The water is fed into large, shallow ponds, where it evaporates and leaves sea salt behind.

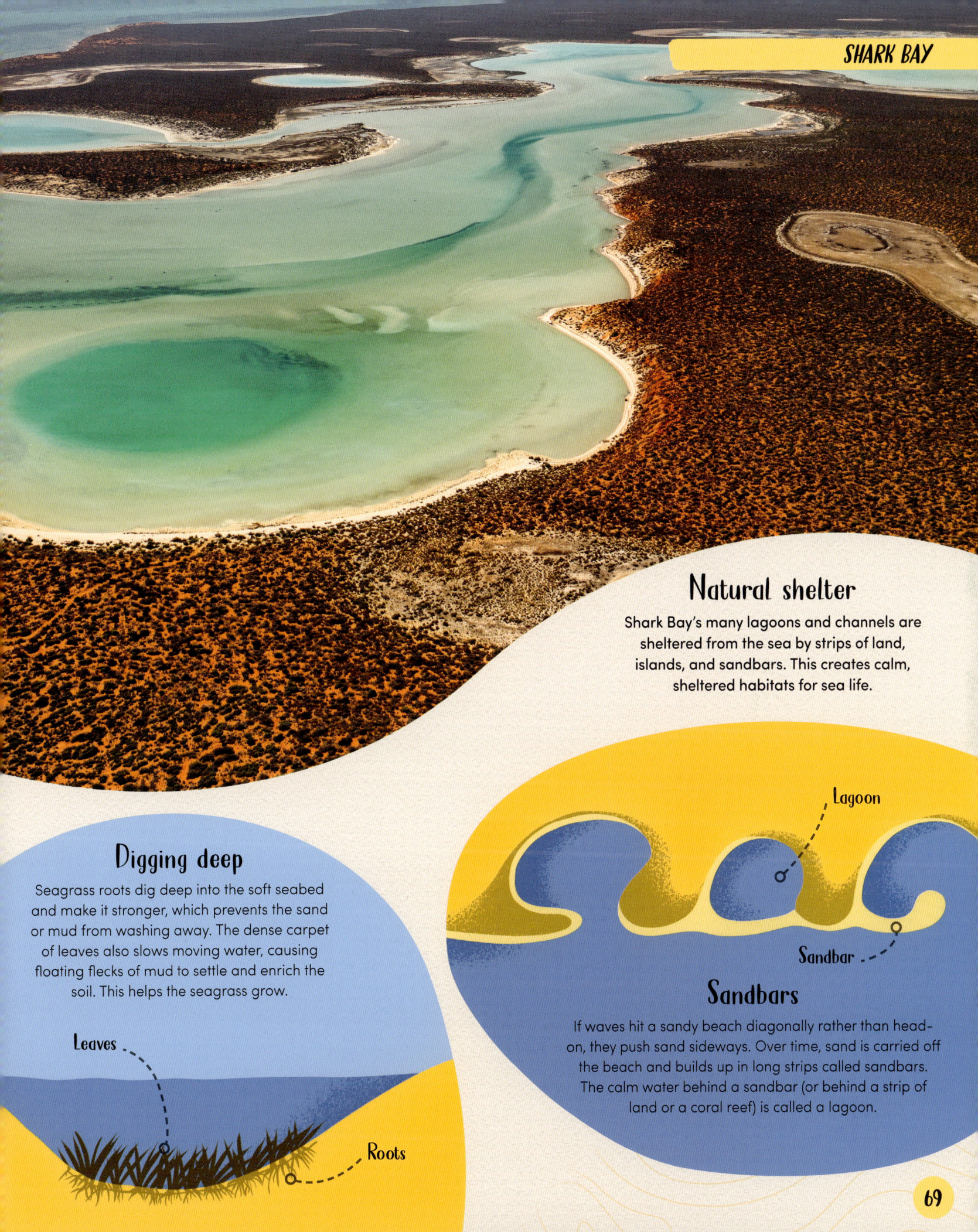

## Natural shelter

Shark Bay's many lagoons and channels are sheltered from the sea by strips of land, islands, and sandbars. This creates calm, sheltered habitats for sea life.

Lagoon

Sandbar

## Digging deep

Seagrass roots dig deep into the soft seabed and make it stronger, which prevents the sand or mud from washing away. The dense carpet of leaves also slows moving water, causing floating flecks of mud to settle and enrich the soil. This helps the seagrass grow.

Leaves

Roots

## Sandbars

If waves hit a sandy beach diagonally rather than head-on, they push sand sideways. Over time, sand is carried off the beach and builds up in long strips called sandbars. The calm water behind a sandbar (or behind a strip of land or a coral reef) is called a lagoon.

### Loggerhead sea turtle
(*Caretta caretta*)

Loggerhead sea turtles are named for their large heads. They have massive skulls and powerful jaw muscles, which they use to crunch hard-shelled prey such as crabs.

### Egg-eating sea snake
(*Emydocephalus annulatus*)

This sea snake eats mainly fish eggs, which it scrapes off rocks using special scales on its lips. It is venomous, but its venom is fairly weak, so it does not pose a danger to humans.

# Animals of Shark Bay

Shark Bay's shallow, sheltered waters are famous for being a shark hotspot, but over 1,500 other species can also be found here. The bay boasts 240 species of birds, 320 species of fish, 218 species of bivalves, and more than 80 species of corals. It also serves as a refuge for many endangered species, including the loggerhead sea turtle and the dugong.

### Indo-Pacific bottlenose dolphin
(*Tursiops aduncus*)

These blue-gray dolphins are highly intelligent and social creatures. Among the few animals known to use tools, they use marine sponges to protect their snouts when foraging on the seafloor.

## Australian giant cuttlefish
### (Sepia apama)

This is the largest of all cuttlefish, reaching up to 39 in (1 m) long from the top of its head to the tip of its tentacles. Like all cuttlefish, it has three hearts, which pump blue blood around its body.

## Spotted eagle ray
### (Aetobatus narinari)

These speckled sea creatures have venomous spines on their tails that they use for self-defense. They can jump completely out of the water, although no one is certain why they do so.

## Dugong
### (Dugong dugon)

Dugongs are harmless herbivores that sustain themselves on seagrass. These gentle giants can live to 70 years old. They communicate underwater using chirps, whistles, and grunts, much as dolphins do.

## The sharks of Shark Bay

Shark Bay is home to more than 28 species of sharks, including the world's largest, the whale shark.

Western wobbegong

Whale shark

Epaulette shark

Scalloped hammerhead

# Tiger shark

Named for their striped skin and feared by beachgoers around the world, tiger sharks have a reputation for being aggressive predators with a lethal bite. Although these sharks rarely attack humans, the fear people have of them is understandable. Their powerful jaws are strong enough to crack the shell of a sea turtle and they can reach lengths of up to 18 ft (5.5 m). Only one other flesh-eating shark, the fearsome great white, is bigger.

### Lethal teeth

The teeth of tiger sharks have serrated edges like steak knives—perfect for cutting through flesh. They come in handy when these sharks are hunting hard-shelled prey.

## Trash cans

Tiger sharks are sometimes called the trash cans of the sea as they eat anything they find, dead or alive, including crustaceans, turtles, seals, stingrays, and smaller sharks. Seabirds resting on the water are a common snack.

## Night vision

Tiger sharks have excellent night vision. Scientists estimate that their ability to see in low light is 10 times better than our own. A layer of mirrorlike tissue lining the inside of the eyeball amplifies light in dark conditions.

## Built to kill

Although they primarily scavenge their meals, these sharks are excellent hunters. Using tiny electro-sensing organs on their snouts, they can detect the electrical fields of prey hidden in the sand. They can also pick up the scent of blood in the water from hundreds of feet away.

# Plants of Shark Bay

Shark Bay is home to what may be the largest living organism on Earth: a seagrass plant that has spread to cover more than 69 square miles (180 sq km) of the seafloor. This giant is one of a diverse collection of seagrass species that keep the bay's water clean, protect beaches from erosion by waves, and provide food, shelter, and homes to many sea creatures.

### Fern seagrass
*(Halophila spinulosa)*

This fernlike seagrass has up to 20 pairs of leaves on each stem. As it grows, new leaves form from the tip and old leaves fall off the bottom. This species is one of the dugong's favorite foods.

### Ribbonweed
*(Posidonia australis)*

In 2022, scientists reported that a vast patch of this seagrass is a single gigantic plant with interconnected roots. It covers a greater area than any other organism on Earth, making it a top contender for the title of world's largest organism. At 4,500 years old, it is also one of the oldest organisms known.

### Paddle weed
*(Halophila ovalis)*

This fast-growing seagrass gets its name from its wide, paddle-shaped leaves. It is also known as spoon grass and dugong grass because dugongs love it.

## Wire weed
### (Amphibolis antarctica)

Wire weed is the most common seagrass species in Shark Bay. Its green flowers produce seeds that sprout and start growing while still attached to the parent plant, before detaching and floating away to take root elsewhere.

## Noodle seagrass
### (Syringodium isoetifolium)

Noodle seagrass has long, noodle-shaped leaves that can grow to 20 in (50 cm) long. Its leaves contain air pockets that keep them pointing upward.

## Plants and algae

Seagrasses aren't seaweeds—they are flowering plants related to the lilies and grasses that live on land. Like land plants, seagrasses have roots, leaves with veins, flowers, and seeds. Seaweeds, however, belong to a group of simpler organisms called algae. Algae only live in water as they can't support themselves on land.

### Seaweed (alga)

Blades (also called fronds) have no veins.

Holdfast clings to seabed.

### Seagrass (plant)

Leaves have veins to transport substances.

Roots grow into sand or mud.

75

# Big Lagoon

Shark Bay's Big Lagoon features a series of tranquil pools filled with shallow turquoise water. These pools are fed by the sea, but banks of seagrass restrict the flow of water, and the desert climate causes a high rate of evaporation. As a result, the pools are saltier than the sea but they still act as nursery grounds for fish and crustaceans, as well as attracting sharks, turtles, and dolphins.

# The open ocean

Far from land is the open ocean. This immense blue habitat can seem like a desert compared to coastal habitats as life is less abundant. Even so, many organisms make it their home. The open ocean is divided into vertical zones based on sunlight. The sunlit zone at the top is full of energy and life, while the zones below are darker, colder, and emptier. The deepest zones are home to some of Earth's strangest animals, from glow-in-the-dark jellyfish to monstrous angler fish that use dangling lights to lure their prey.

**Area**
4 million km²
(1.5 million miles²)

**Depth**
5,000-15,000 ft
(1,500-4,500 m)

**Coastline**
None

# Sargasso Sea

## In the heart of the Atlantic Ocean lies the Sargasso Sea.

This mysterious and vibrant region differs from other parts of the Atlantic because it's covered by thick mats of a floating brown seaweed called sargassum. The Sargasso Sea is in the center of a swirling current that collects and concentrates sargassum, as well as plastics and other floating debris.

THE FIRST KNOWN RECORD OF THE SARGASSO SEA WAS WRITTEN BY CHRISTOPHER COLUMBUS IN 1492.

NORTH AMERICA

### Sargassum

Unlike most seaweeds, which spend their lives anchored to the seafloor, sargassum floats around freely in the ocean. It keeps itself afloat using gas-filled balls on its branches.

The frog fish is camouflaged to look like sargassum.

SARGASSO
SEA

Sargasso
Sea

SOUTH
AMERICA

## Seaweed mats

Mats of sargassum can stretch for miles across the ocean. They provide food and shelter to a wide variety of marine species including shrimps, crabs, fish, and seabirds. Some animals spend their whole lives among the floating seaweed.

# Geography of the Sargasso Sea

The Sargasso Sea is a sea within an ocean. It is the only sea in the world whose boundaries aren't defined by land, but by ocean currents. From above, it looks like an endless expanse of flat, featureless ocean. However, the Sargasso Sea is full of life, and its seafloor is a dynamic landscape peppered with undersea volcanoes.

## Open water

Seen from above, drifts of sargassum look like a brown stain in the water. These patches of sargassum expand in summer before breaking up in winter storms. Dead sargassum sometimes piles up on beaches in Florida and the Bahamas, where it rots and stinks like rotten eggs.

## Vertical migration

Every night, open-ocean habitats such as the Sargasso Sea host the largest migration on Earth. Under the cover of darkness, billions of tiny animals (zooplankton) move up into the shallows to feed on tiny plantlike organisms (phytoplankton). This massive up-and-down movement of life is known as the diel vertical migration.

At night the zooplankton swim up to the surface to feed on phytoplankton.

At dawn the zooplankton return to deeper waters to hide from predators.

## Ocean currents

Swirling currents trap water at the center of the Sargasso Sea for up to 50 years at a time. These rotating currents are called gyres. They are created by global wind patterns and Earth's rotation, and can be found in all five of our planet's oceans.

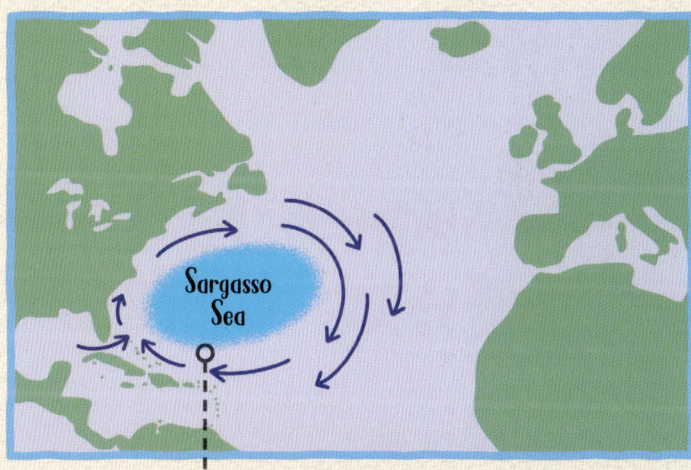

Rotating gyres trap water and sargassum in place, forming the Sargasso Sea.

## Clear blue water

The Sargasso Sea is famous for its crystal clear waters. On a good day, someone at the surface can see 200 ft (60 m) deep. The unusual clarity is because there are low levels of phytoplankton (microscopic plantlike organisms) in the water.

## Still waters

The waters of the Sargasso Sea are sometimes so still that their surface looks like a mirror. In 1492, Christopher Columbus's ship, the *Santa María*, got stranded in the Sargasso Sea for 21 days. It wasn't the seaweed that trapped the ship, but the lack of strong winds.

83

### Sargassum swimming crab
### (Portunus sayi)

When the sargassum swimming crab isn't using its flattened hind legs to swim, it's hanging out on a mat of floating sargassum. These crabs have been known to hitch rides on the backs of loggerhead turtles.

# Animals of the Sargasso Sea

The floating seaweed of the Sargasso provides food and shelter for hundreds of species, from sharks and flying fish to baby turtles and crabs. Many animals spawn or give birth here, where their vulnerable young will be relatively safe.

### Portuguese man-o-war
### (Physalia physalis)

This floating deathtrap kills small fish and other animals with stinging tentacles. It looks like a jellyfish but is only distantly related. Its body is actually a colony of many clones that hang from a gas-filled bag, which acts as both a float and a sail.

### Sargassum frogfish
### (Histrio histrio)

With frilly fins and the ability to change color, hiding among the sargassum is no problem for the frogfish. It is an ambush predator, hiding until prey comes close and then sucking the victim into its huge, froglike mouth by jetting water out of its gills.

# Sea turtle nursery

Many turtles rely on sargassum as youngsters, including green turtles, loggerhead turtles, and the critically endangered hawksbill and Kemp's Ridley turtles. Baby turtles hide from predators in the sargassum and sometimes snack on it.

## Atlantic flying fish
### (Cheilopogon melanurus)

Flying fish lay their bright-orange eggs in the sargassum. They are often seen flying across the water's surface, to avoid predators in the water, though they sometimes get snatched in mid-air by seabirds. Their streamlined shape helps them gather enough speed underwater to propel themselves to the surface, and their large, winglike fins get them airborne.

## Dolphin fish
### (Coryphaena hippurus)

Sargassum provides a safe space for many young fish to grow up, including dolphin fish. Dolphin fish have long, sleek bodies with heavy, sloping foreheads. They are not related to the dolphins they are named after.

## Porbeagle shark
### (Lamna nasus)

Porbeagle sharks give birth in the Sargasso Sea, sometimes travelling more than 1,200 miles (2,000 km) to do so. It's believed that this shark's name originates from the combination of the words "porpoise" and "beagle," a reference to its porpoiselike body shape and impressive hunting skills.

# European eel

For years, scientists had no idea where European eels came from. They saw adult eels leave rivers in Europe and venture into the sea. A few months later, young eels swam back. Scientists assumed the eels traveled somewhere in the Atlantic Ocean to breed, but exactly where was a mystery.

## Adult eels

Long-bodied and long-lived, European eels can grow 4.3 ft (1.3 m) long and can live to 85 years old. They spend most of their lives in rivers and estuaries and only venture into the ocean to breed. Once breeding is complete, the adult eels die.

## Yellow eel

After a while in freshwater, elvers' bellies turn yellow and they grow to over 3 ft (1 m) long. Eels spend most of their lives in this form.

## Silver eel

As eels mature their eyes grow, their bellies turn white, and their sides become silver. They leave rivers and swim to the Sargasso Sea.

Crossing the Atlantic

## Elver

On reaching freshwater, glass eels grow into elvers. These are twice the size and no longer transparent.

Ocean    River

# Journey of a lifetime

Eels travel up to 6,200 miles (10,000 km) to breed in the Sargasso Sea. They go through a series of remarkable transformations along the way.

## Spawning

Scientists are sure that European eels mate in the Sargasso Sea, but no one has ever seen it happen.

## Eggs

After the eggs are fertilized, ocean currents carry them east to Europe. They will hatch after just two days.

## Glass eel

After several months, the leptocephali become glass eels. Their shape is now tubular, not flat.

## Leptocephali

The eggs hatch into tiny flat larvae called leptocephali, which are only a fraction of an inch long.

# Strong instincts

Once adult eels start to migrate to the sea, their instincts are so strong that nothing gets in their way. They will even drag themselves out of the water and over land to reach their destination.

# Glass eels

During their journey to freshwater, leptocephali grow into small, see-through forms known as glass eels. Eel farmers grow glass eels into adults they can sell, and illegal poaching of glass eels is one of the reasons this species is critically endangered.

# Larval life forms

As larvae, European eels are known as leptocephali, which means "slim head" in ancient Greek. These leaflike larvae hatch out from eggs laid in the Sargasso Sea. Once hatched, they swim back across the Atlantic, toward Europe.

## Cyanobacteria

These microscopic organisms can photosynthesize like plants but are much more ancient. They have been living in the sea for 3.5 billion years, making them the oldest known life forms on Earth.

## Not plant or animal

Neither plant, animal, nor fungus, dinoflagellates belong to a kingdom of single-celled organisms known as protists. They can photosynthesize, as plants do, but also hunt and eat other organisms, as animals do.

# Plankton of the Sargasso Sea

You couldn't tell by looking at it, but the Sargasso Sea is teeming with plankton. There are more of these tiny plants (phytoplankton) and animals (zooplankton) in the ocean than there are stars in the night sky. Plankton form the base of marine food chains, supporting everything from barnacles to blue whales. Phytoplankton are not true plants but do a similar job, harvesting energy from the Sun in a process called photosynthesis.

## Copepods

These tiny crustaceans (crab relatives) are the most abundant animals in the ocean. Copepods have one eye, two antennae, and a segmented body. They are eaten by a wide variety of creatures including fish, squid, whales, and other copepods.

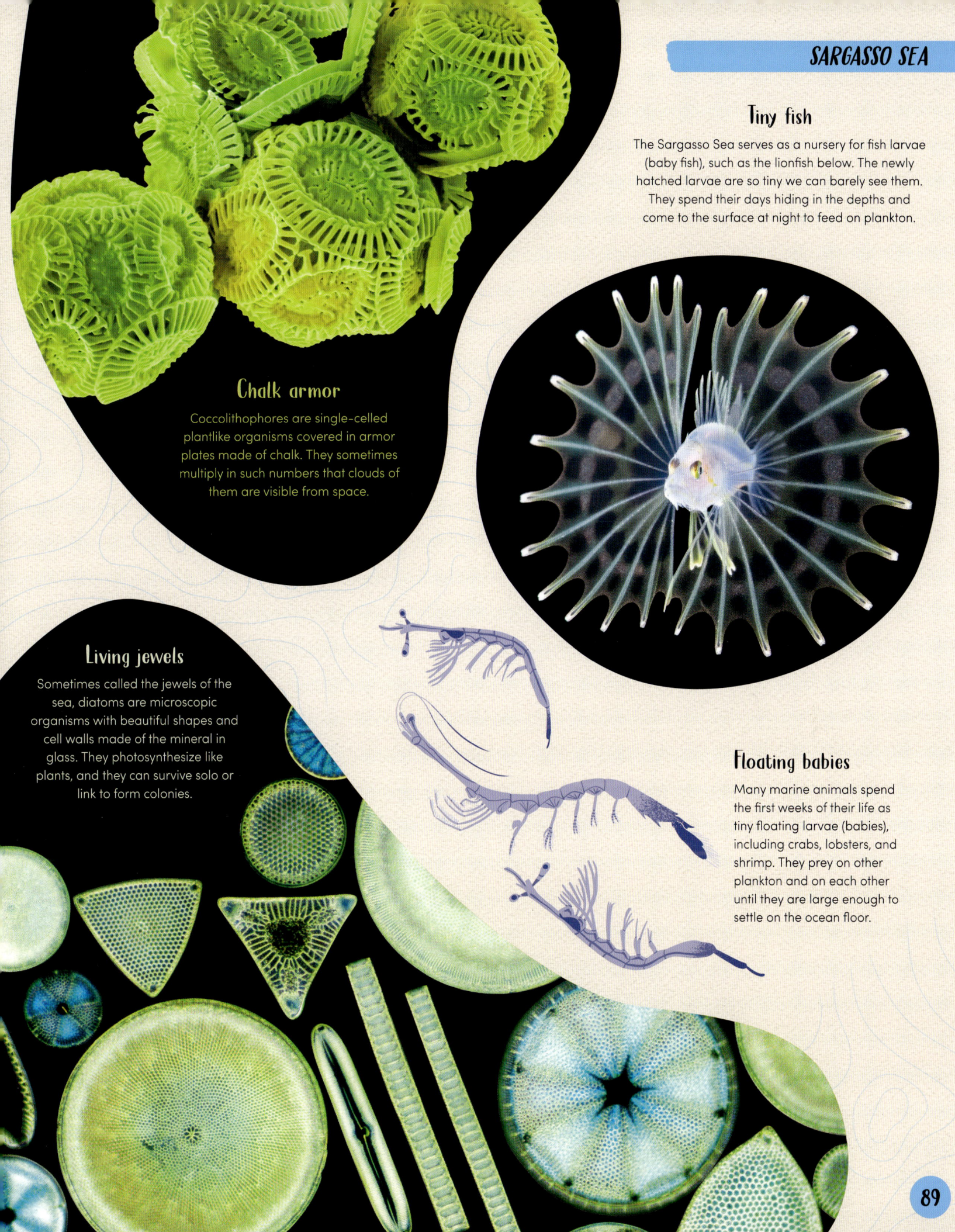

## Tiny fish

The Sargasso Sea serves as a nursery for fish larvae (baby fish), such as the lionfish below. The newly hatched larvae are so tiny we can barely see them. They spend their days hiding in the depths and come to the surface at night to feed on plankton.

## Chalk armor

Coccolithophores are single-celled plantlike organisms covered in armor plates made of chalk. They sometimes multiply in such numbers that clouds of them are visible from space.

## Living jewels

Sometimes called the jewels of the sea, diatoms are microscopic organisms with beautiful shapes and cell walls made of the mineral in glass. They photosynthesize like plants, and they can survive solo or link to form colonies.

## Floating babies

Many marine animals spend the first weeks of their life as tiny floating larvae (babies), including crabs, lobsters, and shrimp. They prey on other plankton and on each other until they are large enough to settle on the ocean floor.

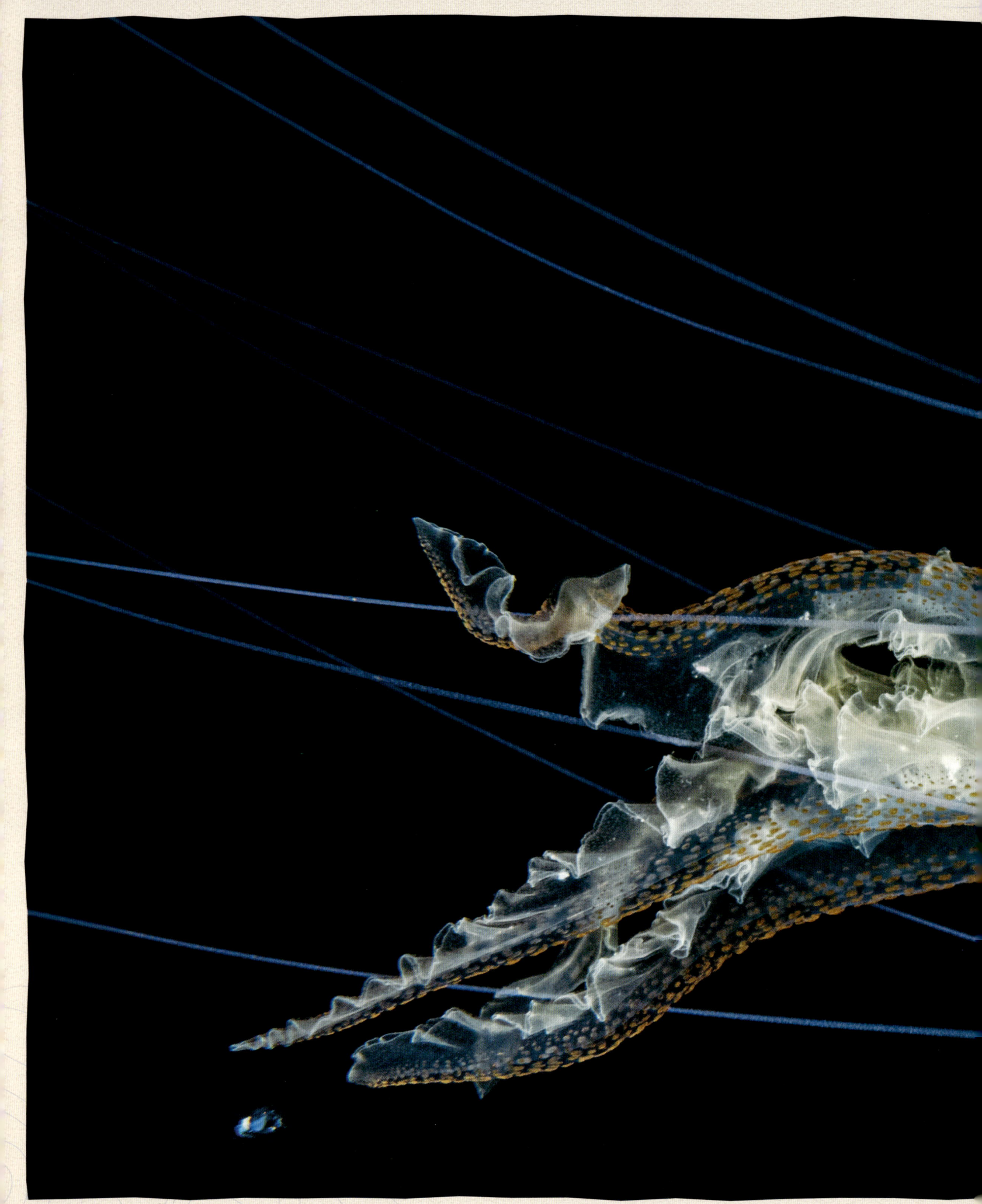

# Brainless wonders

Jellyfish have been cruising the seas since long before dinosaurs existed. They move by squeezing water out of their bell-shaped body, which pushes them forward. They have no heads, brains, eyes, or ears, but a simple net of nerve cells allows them to react to light and prey, which they catch with stinging tentacles. This species, called the mauve stinger, produces flashes of light as a defense when it senses danger.

**Length**
1,580 miles (2,550 km)

**Deepest point**
6.8 miles (10.9 km)

**Age**
180 million years

# Mariana Trench

This, vast crescent-shaped crack in Earth's crust is the site of the deepest point on our planet.

Hidden far beneath the surface of the Pacific Ocean, south of Japan, lies a long, deep valley in the ocean floor: the Mariana Trench. Its record-breaking depths are pitch black, cold, and under immense pressure. Despite these extreme conditions, all manner of creatures can be found living here. Many of them defy imagination.

## Marine snow

Many deep-sea animals feed on "marine snow"—dead plankton, feces, and bits of dead animals that slowly sink to the seafloor like snowflakes.

92

Asia

Australia

PHILIPPINE SEA

## Seabed gardens

Colonies of corals live around the Mariana Trench. Unlike the corals in shallow waters, deep-sea corals don't need sunlight to survive. They feed on microscopic organisms that they catch with their sticky tentacles.

Mariana Trench

## Challenger Deep

The deepest part of the Mariana Trench is called Challenger Deep. Scientists have explored this area using submersibles. This photo shows volcanic rocks covering the seafloor.

# Geography of the Mariana Trench

The Mariana Trench stretches for 1,580 miles (2,550 km) across the bottom of the Pacific Ocean. As well as being pitch black, it is very cold at the bottom of this steep-sided valley, with temperatures a few degrees above freezing. Because of the cold, deep-sea animals here move and breathe slowly.

## Under pressure

The bottom of the Mariana Trench is one of the most extreme environments on Earth. The pressure here is immense—the equivalent of 100 elephants standing on your head. Despite the hostile conditions, the trench teems with life.

## Deepest point

The Mariana Trench was discovered by explorers aboard the British ship HMS *Challenger* in 1875. They measured the trench's depth by throwing weighted ropes over the side and estimated its deepest point to be 5.1 miles (8.2 km). It wasn't until 1951 that another ship, *Challenger II*, used sonar to work out the exact maximum depth and found it to be nearly 1.9 miles (3 km) deeper. The point was named the Challenger Deep in honor of the first ship.

Marine biologists divide the deep sea into different zones depending on how deep and dark it is.

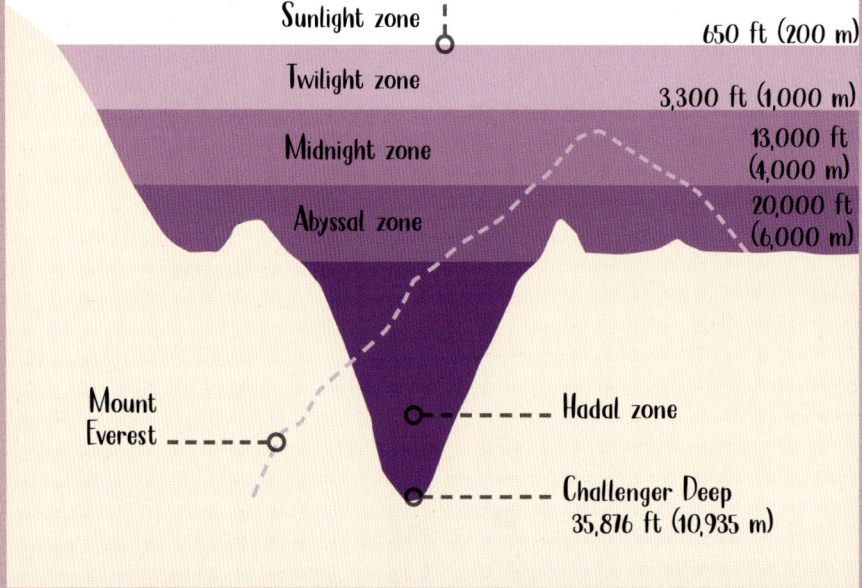

Sunlight zone — 650 ft (200 m)

Twilight zone — 3,300 ft (1,000 m)

Midnight zone — 13,000 ft (4,000 m)

Abyssal zone — 20,000 ft (6,000 m)

Mount Everest

Hadal zone

Challenger Deep
35,876 ft (10,935 m)

Philippine Plate · Mariana Trench · Pacific Plate

## How the trench formed

Earth's crust is made up of huge chunks called tectonic plates, which move very slowly. The Mariana Trench formed when one plate, called the Pacific Plate, slipped beneath its neighbor, the Philippine Plate. This process has been happening for millions of years and continues today, causing the trench to get deeper and deeper.

## Exploration

A total of 27 people have visited Challenger Deep in submersibles. There have also been many uncrewed submersible missions to study the seabed and investigate the strange forms of life that flourish in this hostile environment.

## Slippery seafloor

Swiss oceanographer Jacques Piccard, who piloted the first descent to Challenger Deep in 1960, described the bottom of the trench as being covered in "ooze." Scientists would later discover that the ooze was a mixture of clay and the crushed skeletons of billions of tiny single-celled organisms known as diatoms.

95

# Animals of the Mariana Trench

When scientists first explored the Mariana Trench, they didn't expect to find many animals. They thought the immense pressure, cold, and darkness would make life impossible. However, trips into the trench with submersibles revealed that it abounds with weird and wonderful creatures, including see-through fish and meat-eating sponges.

## Mariana snailfish
### (Pseudoliparis swirei)

Discovered in 2014, this peculiar fish with pale, semitransparent skin lives as deep as 5 miles (8 km). That makes it the world's deepest-living fish. It looks delicate and is barely larger than a human foot, but it's the top predator at its depth, where it feeds on small crustaceans.

## Carnivorous sponges
### (Cladorhizidae)

Most sponges filter the seawater that passes through them for morsels of food. But members of the family Cladorhizidae have a different technique—they trap tiny crustaceans with hooks and spines. Once caught, the struggling prey is enveloped and digested.

## Crossota
### (Hydromedusae)

Each voyage into the depths of the Mariana Trench brings to light species that are new to science. For instance, this jellyfish-relative with a bell like a flying saucer was discovered at a depth of 2.3 miles (3.7 km).

## Sea pigs
### (Scotoplanes)

Sea pigs are among the most abundant animals in the deep sea. They are related to starfish and have 5–7 pairs of feet that they use to creep across the seafloor in search of scraps of food. When a dead whale sinks to the seafloor, hundreds of sea pigs show up to pick the carcass clean.

Upward-facing eyes

## Acorn worm
### (Torquaratoridae)

This worm is nothing like the earthworms you see in garden soil. Its body is like jelly. If you tried to pick one up, it would probably fall apart in your hand. This colorful creature crawls across the seafloor, slurping up mud using a long, tonguelike structure called a proboscis.

## Pacific barreleye fish
### (Macropinna microstoma)

This otherworldly fish has no problem spotting the silhouettes of prey swimming above it, due to its transparent head. Its bright green, supersensitive eyes usually point upward, but they can rotate to look forward too.

## Humpback anglerfish
### (Melanocetus johnsonii)

On top of this fish's head is a fishing rod that ends in a glowing light. By waving this about, the anglerfish attracts prey into striking range. There are more than 200 species of deep-sea anglerfish, each with its own special fishing rod.

97

# Bioluminescence

In the constant darkness of the deep sea, the best way to communicate is with light. That's why most deep-sea creatures have evolved the ability to create their own light from chemicals in their bodies. Sea creatures use this ability, known as bioluminescence, in different ways, including to scare away predators and trick their prey. On land, only fireflies, glowworms, and a handful of other organisms are bioluminescent. But in the ocean depths, 75 percent of species are able to glow.

## Finding mates

Some fish use bioluminescence to help them find mates. Male and female lanternfish produce different patterns of light on their sides. Scientists think that the patterns let the fish pick out a suitable mate in the dark.

## Chemical weapons

A great way to escape from a predator is to squirt it with a cloud of glowing liquid, which is what several kinds of deep-sea fish, shrimp, and squid do. The bioluminescent fluid distracts the hunter for a second, giving the prey a chance to swim away. As a bonus, the predator ends up covered in brightly lit goo—making them a target for their enemies.

## Light-show squid

Few creatures shine as bright as the firefly squid. Its body is covered in thousands of light organs that it can flash all at once or in turns to create complex light shows.

## Counter-illumination

Light that isn't too bright can serve as camouflage. The kitefin shark has lights on its belly to match the blue glow of the sea surface when seen from below in the daytime. This trick is called counter-illumination and hides the fish from both predators and prey.

## Glowing jellyfish

About half of all jellyfish species are bioluminescent. The crystal jellyfish has about 100 tiny light organs around its bell. They emit bright flashes of light when the jellyfish is disturbed, which scares away most predators.

## Photophores

Many bioluminescent animals store the chemicals that produce light in small organs called photophores.

**Size**
582,000 square miles
(1.51 million sq km)

**Deepest point**
Sigsbee Deep, 2.7 miles
(4.4 km) below sea level

**Length of coastline**
3,700 miles (6,000 km)

# Gulf of Mexico

**Covering an area nearly the size of Alaska, the Gulf of Mexico is the world's largest gulf.**

A gulf is a large area of ocean that is almost surrounded by land, like a gigantic mouth. Many of North America's largest rivers flow into the Gulf of Mexico, creating rich wetlands along its coastline. However, wetlands aren't the only thing this gulf is famous for. Just offshore, seagrass meadows, mangrove forests, and coral reefs abound. Dive a little deeper and you can also find mud volcanoes, underwater lakes, and gases seeping out of the seafloor.

### Deep-sea coral

The Gulf of Mexico is one of the few places on Earth where more corals can be found in the deep than in the shallows. It is home to more than 250 species of deep-sea corals, but only around 100 shallow-water corals.

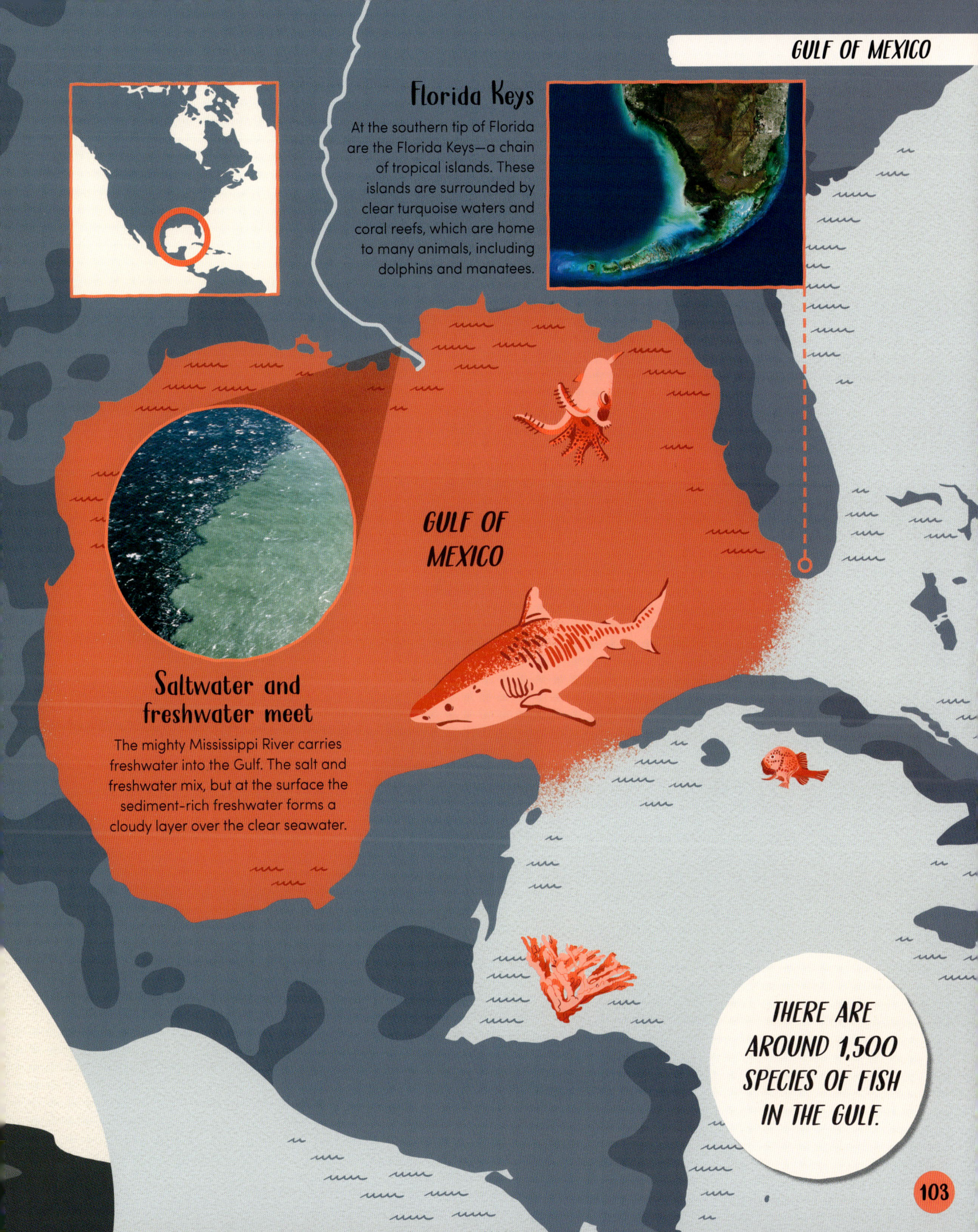

## Florida Keys

At the southern tip of Florida are the Florida Keys—a chain of tropical islands. These islands are surrounded by clear turquoise waters and coral reefs, which are home to many animals, including dolphins and manatees.

## GULF OF MEXICO

## Saltwater and freshwater meet

The mighty Mississippi River carries freshwater into the Gulf. The salt and freshwater mix, but at the surface the sediment-rich freshwater forms a cloudy layer over the clear seawater.

THERE ARE AROUND 1,500 SPECIES OF FISH IN THE GULF.

103

## Mississippi swirls

The Mississippi River carries roughly 500 million tons (450 million tonnes) of sediment into the Gulf of Mexico each year. As the freshwater of the river meets the saltwater of the ocean it forms beautiful sediment swirls, which can be seen from space.

## Hurricanes

Hurricanes become stronger and more dangerous as they travel across warm waters such as those in the Gulf of Mexico. Hundreds of hurricanes have crossed the Gulf over the years, and they are expected to get more powerful as the oceans warm up.

# Geography of the Gulf of Mexico

Surrounded by land on almost all sides, the Gulf of Mexico is shallow around the edges, but gets deeper as you move toward its center. It is alive with activity. On the seafloor, the slow movement of Earth's crust creates geological features such as brine pools and cold seeps. On the surface, warm waters fuel massive hurricanes that batter the coastlines.

# Brine pools

Far below the surface of the Gulf are mysterious underwater lakes known as brine pools. These lakes are nothing like the ones on land. They are up to ten times saltier than the surrounding seawater, and are so full of chemicals that nothing but microbes can survive in them.

# How brine pools form

When salt deposits beneath the seafloor come into contact with seawater they dissolve, creating super-salty water known as brine. Brine is much heavier than seawater so it settles on the seafloor, forming puddles and pools that are deadly to fish.

Seawater is less dense than brine, and there is little current in the deep sea, so the two liquids do not mix.

Cracks in the seafloor expose underground salt deposits to seawater.

# Cold seeps

Cold seeps are places where chemicals such as hydrogen sulfide and methane bubble up from cracks in the seafloor. These energy-rich chemicals support strange ecosystems that have no need for sunlight. Here, a spider crab clambers over mussels and worms feeding at a cold seep.

### Goliath Grouper
#### (Epinephelus itajara)

This gigantic fish is an ambush predator that swallows its prey whole. It opens its huge mouth very quickly, creating a vacuum that sucks in fish and large invertebrates.

### Atlantic bluefin tuna
#### (Thunnus thynnus)

These fast-swimming fish can reach speeds of 40 mph (64 kph), which is faster than a gazelle. This is an impressive speed for a fish that can weigh as much as 1,500 lb (680 kg). Atlantic bluefin tuna lay their eggs in the Gulf of Mexico, and the baby tuna spend the first part of their lives here.

# Animals of the Gulf of Mexico

From its coastal estuaries and coral reefs to its deep-water cold seeps and brine pools, there is no shortage of habitats for animals in the Gulf of Mexico. Around 1,500 species of fish, 395 species of birds, 29 species of marine mammals, and five species of sea turtles spend some or all of their lives in the Gulf. Many birds stop off here, using it as a resting place during their long yearly migrations.

### Elkhorn coral
#### (Acropora palmata)

Named for its antler-shaped branches, elkhorn coral once dominated reefs in the Gulf and Caribbean Sea. However, thanks to a combination of disease outbreaks, climate change, and habitat loss, it is now critically endangered.

## Sperm whale
### (Physeter macrocephalus)

These massive marine mammals are champion divers, capable of diving 10,000 ft (3,000 m) deep and staying there for over an hour. They have massive heads and the biggest brains of any animal.

## Queen conch
### (Lobatus gigas)

Prized for its stunning shell, the queen conch is a large marine snail that can grow to 12 in (30 cm) long. Once it reaches its maximum size, it focuses all of its energy on thickening its shell. The thicker the shell gets, the less vulnerable the conch is to predators.

## Creatures of the deep

Deep down in the ocean live strange-looking creatures that have adapted to survive in cold, dark water under immense pressure.

Dumbo octopus

Vampire squid

## Bull shark
### (Carcharhinus leucas)

This barrel-bodied species can be found in the Gulf's rivers and estuaries, as well as its coastal waters. Its presence in freshwater ecosystems means it encounters people more often than other species of sharks do.

Netdevil anglerfish

# West Indian Manatee

These huge herbivores can be found quietly grazing on seagrass in warm shallow waters from the Gulf of Mexico to the Caribbean. They typically weigh about half a ton and reach 10 ft (3 m) long, but some can grow much bigger. There are two subspecies of West Indian manatees: the Florida manatee and the slightly smaller Antillean manatee.

## Underwater grazing

To maintain their weight, manatees must eat between four and nine percent of their body weight in seagrass every day. They use their strong, flexible lips to pull the seagrass off the seafloor and into their mouths.

## Agile swimmers

Don't let their sausagelike shape fool you—manatees are strong swimmers. They usually float about, but can reach speeds of 15 mph (24 kph) with just a few flaps of their powerful, paddle-shaped tails.

## Breathing at the surface

Manatees are mammals, and, like all mammals, they breathe air. West Indian manatees can hold their breath for up to 20 minutes, but they typically surface every 3–5 minutes. Manatees only inhale through their nostrils, so they only have to stick their snouts up out of the water to breathe.

## Motherly care

Female manatees are pregnant for around 13 months, and usually have just one calf at a time. Once a baby is born, it suckles milk from a pair of nipples hidden behind its mother's flippers. Young manatees nurse for a long time, and stay with their mothers for up to two years.

# Leatherback sea turtle

These massive marine reptiles are found not just in the Gulf of Mexico but throughout the Atlantic, Pacific, and Indian Oceans. They spend nearly their entire lives in the open ocean, where they feed on jellyfish, squid, crustaceans, and seaweed. Leatherbacks are the world's largest sea turtles and the only sea turtles with flexible, leathery shells rather than hard ones. They have existed for more than 100 million years, but are now in danger of extinction.

## A sandy nest

During nesting season, female leatherbacks haul themselves onto sandy beaches and dig holes to lay their eggs in. Each female lays around 100 eggs, then buries them in the sand before returning to sea. They can repeat this process up to ten times in a single season.

## Hatchling horror

Newly hatched turtles face a series of daunting tasks, which only around one in a thousand will survive. To get started, they must dig themselves out of the nest. Next, they face attack from predators: first on the beach and then in the water, as they make their way toward the open ocean.

## Return to the beach

Female leatherbacks crawl onto beaches to lay their eggs. They will travel thousands of miles, sometimes crossing entire oceans, to reach the areas where they hatched.

Leatherbacks can dive deeper than any other turtle, reaching depths of up to 4,000 ft (1,200 m).

## Ocean life

Leatherback sea turtles are built for life in the open ocean. Streamlined bodies and powerful flippers allow them to travel vast distances in the water, while swimming against powerful currents. Males never return to land after hatching, and females only visit land to lay their eggs.

111

# Gentle giants

If you visit the Gulf of Mexico you might be lucky enough to see a whale shark—the world's largest fish. They may be sharks, but these gentle giants pose no danger to humans. They feed on plankton and small fish, which they collect by swallowing water with their vast mouths before sieving it through their gills. Unlike most sharks, whale sharks have no eyelids. Instead their eyes are covered in hundreds of tiny teeth for protection.

# Coastal habitats

The most varied marine habitats of all are where land meets the sea. Coastal habitats include tide pools, sandy beaches, muddy estuaries, mangrove swamps, and towering cliffs that are pounded by waves. Many of the animals that live here lead amphibious lives, which means they spend part their life underwater and the other part on land.

FACT FILE

**Area**
4,000 square miles
(10,300 sq km)

**Age**
7,000 years

**Dominant species**
Sundari mangrove
tree

# Sundarbans mangrove forest

**Straddling India and Bangladesh, the Sundarbans region is the world's largest mangrove forest.**

Also called a mangrove swamp, a mangrove forest is a special kind of forest found on tropical and subtropical coasts. Unlike normal trees, which take root in solid ground, mangroves grow in unstable ground such as muddy riverbanks or sandy coasts. They stabilize the coastline, protecting it from storms. The dense mangrove forest of the Sundarbans is home to a unique mix of aquatic animals and land animals, from crocodiles and dolphins to monkeys and tigers.

## What are mangroves?

Mangroves are trees and shrubs with dense, evergreen leaves and stiltlike roots that hold them well above the water. They have special features to survive in salty water, waterlogged mud, and tides that continually rise and fall.

India

Bangladesh

Sundarbans

Bay of Bengal

India

## Wildlife haven

The roots of mangrove trees form a dense thicket along the coast, creating a safe haven for small sea creatures to hide from bigger predators. Many ocean fish use mangrove forests as nurseries for their eggs and young.

117

# Geography of the Sundarbans

The Sundarbans are more than just mangroves. Fed by the outflow of the Ganges, Brahmaputra, and Meghna Rivers, this vast and diverse ecosystem contains dozens of interconnected estuaries, mudflats, creeks, and islands. Storms and a whopping 11.5 feet (3.5 m) of rain a year drench this region, making this wetland even wetter.

## Seen from space

Satellite images reveal how water flows through the Sundarbans. After passing through farmland, water makes its way through the dense mangrove forests, which appear as dark zones in this image. The pale areas in the sea are rich in sediment carried by the rivers.

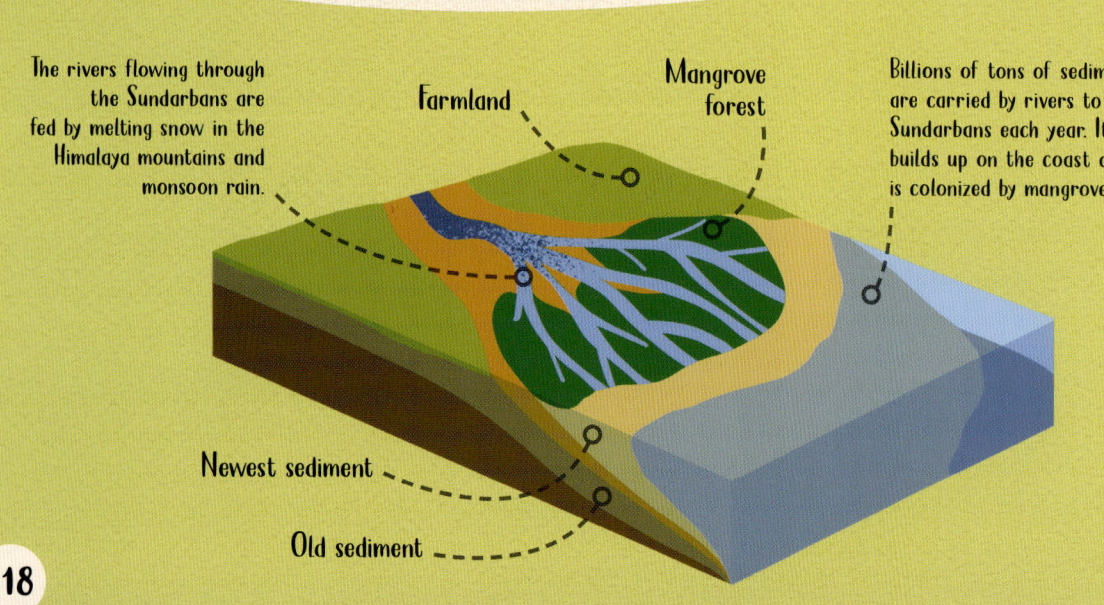

The rivers flowing through the Sundarbans are fed by melting snow in the Himalaya mountains and monsoon rain.

Farmland

Mangrove forest

Billions of tons of sediment are carried by rivers to the Sundarbans each year. It builds up on the coast and is colonized by mangroves.

Newest sediment

Old sediment

## How the Sundbarbans formed

Over thousands of years, sediment (mud and sand) carried by rivers created a large delta—a new area of land that extends into the sea. Mangrove trees soon took root in the nutrient-rich mud. The trees stabilized the land, creating the Sundarbans we know today.

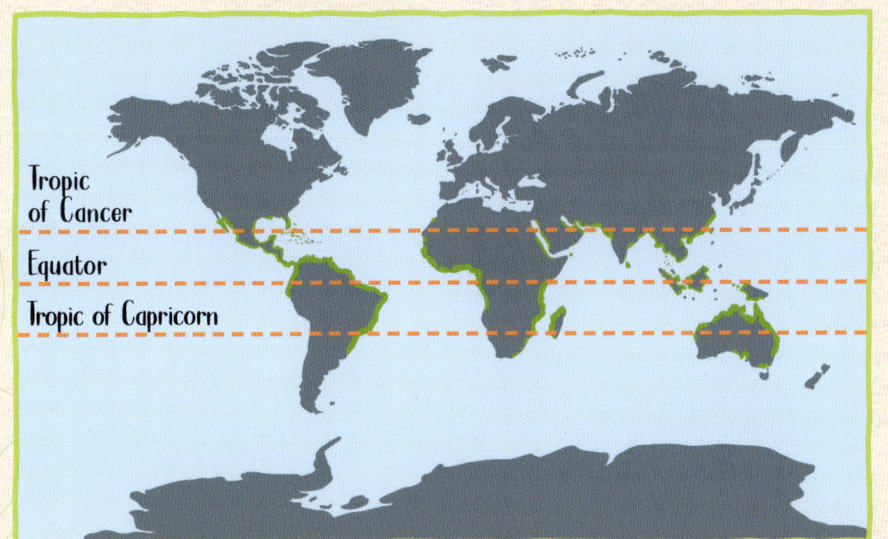

Tropic
of Cancer

Equator

Tropic of Capricorn

## Tropical coastlines

Mangrove forests cannot withstand freezing temperatures, so they can live only in tropical and subtropical regions, on either side of the equator. The forests are found on the coasts of over 100 countries, providing coastal protection and habitats for countless species.

## Coastal defense

Mangrove forests protect coastlines from erosion (wearing away) by the sea. The trees' roots hold onto soil, preventing it from being washed away. The trunks and branches take the brunt of the wind and waves created by storms, including powerful cyclones.

### Lesser adjutant
#### (Leptoptilos javanicus)

With its bald head and neck, this large member of the stork family may look as if it scavenges for carrion (dead animals) like a vulture. However, the lesser adjutant prefers to hunt for fish, reptiles, and other small animals. It uses its stiltlike legs to wade and its long bill to snatch prey from the water.

### Fiddler crabs
#### (Uca spp.)

Fiddler crabs come in a variety of colors, including red, blue, and yellow. Males have one regular-sized claw and one giant claw, which they use to impress females. These crabs dig vast networks of tunnels in the muddy banks to hide from predators and keep cool on hot days.

# Animals of the Sundarbans

The mangroves of the Sundarbans have a wealth of animal species. Mammals include the Bengal tiger (the Sundarbans's top predator), otters, dolphins, deer, and macaque monkeys. There are also hundreds of species of birds, reptiles, and fish—as well as countless invertebrates and even a few amphibians. They are all adapted to life in the dense mangrove forest.

### Saltwater crocodile
#### (Crocodylus porosus)

The world's largest reptile, the saltwater crocodile is equally at home in freshwater and seawater thanks to glands on its tongue that excrete (get rid of) salt. It is an ambush predator, lurking in the water until prey come close enough to bite. It swallows small animals whole but tears larger prey into bite-sized pieces by spinning violently in the water.

## Forest dolphins

The Sundarbans are home to a few species of dolphin and porpoise. These aquatic mammals feed on the abundant supply of fish and shrimp, which humans also harvest. Because of this, the dolphins often become entangled in fishing nets.

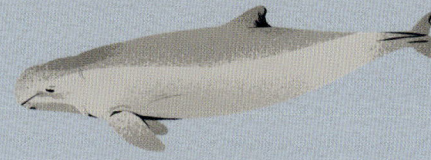

Irrawaddy dolphin
(*Orcaella brevirostris*)

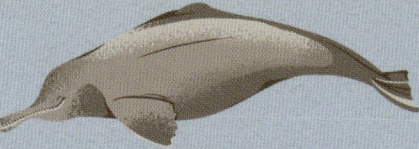

Ganges river dolphin
(*Platanista gangetica*)

Indo-Pacific humpback dolphin
(*Sousa chinensis*)

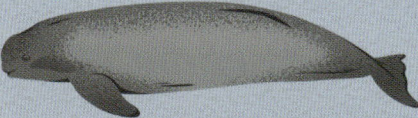

Indo-Pacific finless porpoise
(*Neophocaena phocaenoides*)

## Black-capped kingfisher
### (*Halcyon pileata*)

Perching above the water, the black-capped kingfisher dives when it spots a fish, snapping it up in its bright-red beak. It also eats frogs and large insects. Males and females look similar, and they nest in tunnels, which they dig out of riverbanks.

## Banded archerfish
### (*Toxotes jaculatrix*)

When the banded archerfish cannot find food in the water, it looks above the surface. Its mouth can produce a jet of water powerful enough to knock insects crawling on overhanging branches into the water. The fish then quickly gobbles them up. Banded archerfish can shoot their jets as far as 5 ft (1.5 m).

## Mangrove red snapper
### (*Lutjanus argentimaculatus*)

This fish grows up in the safety of the mangroves but moves out to sea as an adult. It is a predator with sharp teeth and lurks among the mangrove roots waiting to ambush smaller fish and other prey. Mangrove red snappers can reach 39 in (100 cm) in length and 30 lb (14 kg) in weight.

### Fins for walking

When walking on land, a mudskipper uses its pelvic fins, under the front of its body, to prop itself up and its pectoral fins, at the sides of its body, to drag itself forward. The fish can move with surprising speed and can jump as far as 24 in (60 cm), which is more than twice their body length.

The pectoral fins double as legs.

# Mudskipper

Mudskippers are among the most extraordinary fish on Earth, able to walk on land and survive out of water for days at a time. Some can even climb trees. Their ability to move about and breathe both underwater and on land allows these fish to cope with the extreme tidal changes in the Sundarbans.

### Home builders

Mudskippers are industrious workers. The males dig deep burrows in the mud, which serve as protection from predators and rising tides. When a male's burrow is complete, he invites a female to visit and lay hundreds of eggs, which the male then looks after.

## Bulging eyes

Mudskippers have bulging eyes at the top of the head. The eyes can move independently of one another, giving the fish all-round vision. The eyes are also retractable—they can be sucked into the head every few seconds to keep them moist.

## Amphibious fish

Like other fish, mudskippers use their gills to breathe in water. When on land, they use their skin to breathe too—like amphibians (frogs and salamanders) do. Mudskippers need to keep their skin moist for it to absorb oxygen from the air. To use their gills on land, they trap water in the gill chambers, which makes them look like they're puffing out their cheeks.

Mudskippers develop colorful spots in the mating season to attract partners.

Gill chamber

## Stilt roots

One of the most noticeable features of a mangrove forest is the mass of roots that branch out in all directions from the lower trunks of the trees. These are called stilt roots and they support the trees. They also prevent the trees from being uprooted when the tides roll in and out.

## Trees with knees

Many species of mangrove tree have knee roots, which arch out of the soil before burrowing back in. These aerial (above-ground) roots have small openings through which air can enter and travel down to the roots in the oxygen-poor soil.

# Plants of the Sundarbans

Plants reign supreme in the Sundarbans. The lush, dense forest is home to a wide variety of mangrove tree species and hundreds of other plants. Even though the soil in the Sundarbans is waterlogged, salty, and poor in oxygen, the plants here have evolved amazing ways to overcome these challenges and flourish.

## Aerial roots

Some mangrove trees have loads of aerial roots that grow upward out of the soil. These roots have openings for air, helping the underground parts of the roots get oxygen. They sometimes contain the green pigment chlorophyll, which allows them to make food by photosynthesis.

## Aquatic palm

The mangrove palm is the only species of palm that can survive in a mangrove ecosystem. Its trunk grows underground. But that doesn't mean the plant is short—its fronds (divided leaves) can reach 30 ft (9 m) in height.

## Salt glands

Mangrove trees have adapted to live in water with salt levels that would kill most plants. Many trees cope by excreting (getting rid of) excess salt through glands in their leaves. This salt can often be seen as crystals on the bottom of the leaves.

## Propagules

Some mangroves have special seeds called propagules, which sprout and start growing while still on the tree. Then they drop into the water and float away, before lodging in mud and taking root. Dispersing in the water allows mangrove seeds to reach suitable new habitats.

## Floating cannonballs

The fruit of the cannonball mangrove is a round capsule up to 5 in (12 cm) across. When ripe, the fruit explodes, dispersing the seeds inside it far and wide. Fruits can float and travel for long distances before washing up on distant shores and sprouting there.

## Waxy leaves

Most mangrove trees have a thick waxy substance covering their leaves. It keeps them waterproof at high tides and prevents them from drying out in hot weather.

# Baby shark

Several kinds of sharks—including bull sharks, reef sharks, and the lemon shark seen here in the Bahamas—use mangroves as nurseries. The dense roots and the shallow water provide protection from larger sharks, and the abundant wildlife allows the shark pups to practice hunting before they venture into the open ocean.

**Length of coastline**
About 64,000 miles
(103,000 km)

**Number of islands**
More than 43,000

**Sea temperature**
Summer 75°F (24°C)
Winter 54°F (12°C)

# Rocky coast
# of Patagonia

At the bottom of South America is a region called Patagonia. Its long rocky coastline is one of the world's last unspoiled wildernesses.

Patagonia's mountainous coast has so many craggy inlets and islands that its total length, by some estimates, is greater than the coastline of Australia. This is a land of towering cliffs and rocky bays that are battered by storms, waves, and ever-changing tides. Despite the tough conditions, rocky coastlines like this provide many opportunities for wildlife, from blue whales and other giants of the sea to the many small creatures that make tide pools and beaches their home.

### Clifftop nests

Cormorants and rock shags nest on cliffs, where most predators can't reach them. These diving birds plunge up to 200 ft (60 m) deep in the sea to catch anchovies and octopuses.

South America

MORE THAN 1.7 MILLION PENGUINS LIVE ON THE COAST OF PATAGONIA.

## Deadly waters

Rocks, tides, powerful currents, and stormy weather all make Patagonia's coast dangerous for ships. Much of the coast is still uncharted. Very few people live here, which makes the coast a haven for wildlife.

## Island refuges

The southern tip of Patagonia is a cluster of hundreds of islands. Most are uninhabited and protected. The unspoiled seas around them teem with large mammals, including at least seven whale species.

# Geography of the Patagonian coast

On the west coast of Patagonia, the Andes Mountains meet the Pacific Ocean. The landscape here is dramatic, with snowcapped mountains, deep fjords, and hundreds of rocky islands. Patagonia's east coast is on the Atlantic Ocean. It is flatter and has a drier climate, but deep-ocean currents bring nutrients to the sea surface, supporting an abundance of life.

## Carved by ice

Fjords are narrow but deep bodies of water that are surrounded by steep hills on three sides and connected to the sea. Fjords formed in the ice age when glaciers (rivers of ice) carved out deep valleys as they flowed from mountains to the sea.

## Sea cliffs

The never-ending pounding of waves eats away at (erodes) rocky coastlines, creating cliffs. Sometimes you can see different layers of rock (called strata) in cliffs. These layers formed many millions of years ago. The oldest layers are at the bottom and the youngest layers are on top.

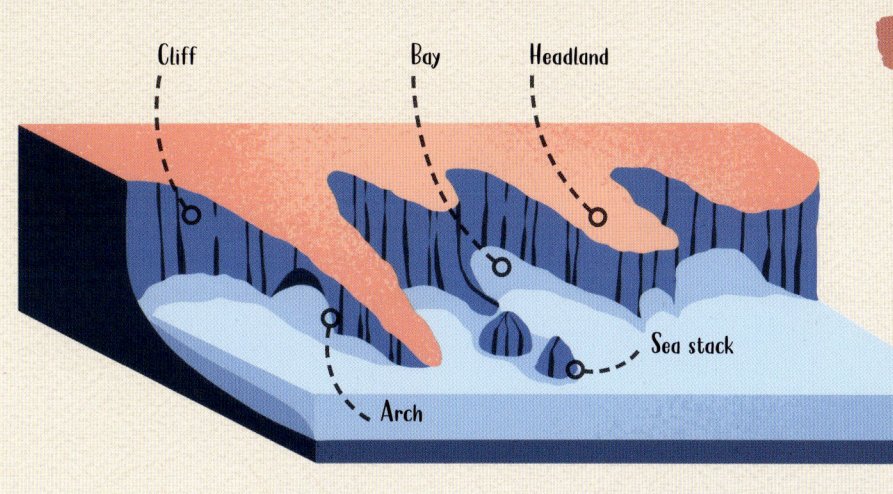

Cliff    Bay    Headland

Sea stack

Arch

# Features of rocky coasts

Erosion by waves carves rocky coastlines into a series of bays and headlands. Waves erode the base of cliffs fastest, creating caves and arches. If an arch collapses, it leaves a column of rock standing in the sea—a sea stack.

# Tide pools

Tide pools are nooks and crannies that collect water as the tide goes out, providing homes for animals like anemones, crabs, sea urchins, barnacles, and mussels. All these animals can hold on tight to rocks so that incoming waves don't wash them out of their pools.

# Tidal zones

The part of a coast that's underwater at high tide but above water at low tide is called the intertidal zone. Different animals live in different parts of the intertidal zone. Barnacles live highest as they can withstand being out of water longest. Starfish and seaweeds live lower down as they can only survive drying out for short periods.

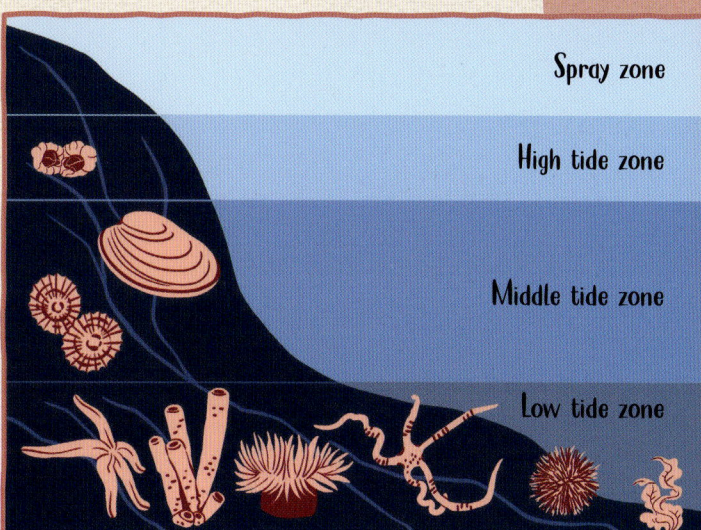

Spray zone

High tide zone

Middle tide zone

Low tide zone

## Marine otter
### (Lontra felina)

Not to be confused with the much larger sea otter of the North Pacific, the marine otter is the smallest marine mammal and lives only in South America. Rarely seen, it avoids sandy beaches and prefers craggy bays and caves. Pups sometimes ride on their mother's belly while she swims on her back.

## Southern right whale
### (Eubalaena australis)

This stocky whale has an unusually large head that takes up a third of its body length. The head is covered with rough patches of skin known as callosities. Barnacles and tiny crustaceans live in the callosities, but the whale doesn't seem to mind.

## Orca
### (Orcinus orca)

The orcas in Patagonia's Peninsula Valdes have a unique hunting strategy that makes use of the steeply sloping beaches. The orcas slide onto the beach to catch young sea lion pups, then ride the retreating waves back into the sea.

# Animals of the Patagonian coast

The waters around Patagonia are rich in the nutrients that plankton need to grow. The plankton provide food for small animals such as fish, which in turn are eaten by whales, sea lions, otters, and seabirds. Many of these large sea creatures breed on the rocky coast, where they are safe from ocean predators and undisturbed by humans.

## Patagonian sea lion
*(Otaria flavescens)*

These are the largest of all the sea lions. Males, which are much larger than females, can weigh 770 lb (350 kg). In December and January, thousands of Patagonian sea lions come ashore to breed, taking over Patagonia's beaches.

## Commerson's dolphin
*(Tonina overa)*

Also known as the panda dolphin, Commerson's dolphin is born gray but turns black and white as it ages. It is famously curious and often approaches passing boats. The Commerson's dolphin is one of the smallest dolphin species, reaching only 5.9 ft (1.8 m) as an adult.

## Penguins

Six species of penguins live in Patagonia. They form large groups, called colonies, on the coast. The biggest colony is in eastern Argentina and has around 400,000 Magellanic penguins.

Macaroni penguin

Gentoo penguin

Southern rockhopper penguin

Humboldt penguin

Magellanic penguin

King penguin

# Southern elephant seal

The southern elephant seal is the largest of all seals, with males stretching up to 20 ft (6 m) long and weighing up to 37 tons, which is as heavy as an elephant. These seals are among the best divers in the ocean. They can reach depths of 4,700 ft (1,430 m) and can stay underwater for two hours. Scientists recently discovered that elephant seals sometimes even take 10-minute power naps during their dives.

## Success story

Southern elephant seals were hunted to the brink of extinction for their blubber (fat), which people used for lamp oil. However, thanks to protection across their range, there are now roughly 600,000 alive today.

## Beach masters

Each breeding season, male elephant seals fight to become master of the beach. Males stab one another in the neck with their large canine teeth until one of them gives up. The winner gets to breed with a group of up to 50 females.

## Warm in winter

The sea off the coast of Patagonia can get very cold in winter, but elephant seals like this female stay warm thanks to a thick layer of blubber. This store of energy also sustains them during the breeding season, when they are unable to hunt.

## Inflatable nose

The name "elephant" doesn't just refer to the great size of these animals. It is also a reference to the male's inflatable, trunklike nose. In the breeding season, males fill their trunks with air and make a drumlike noise to show off to rivals and mates.

# Wandering albatross

With the largest wingspan of any bird, the wandering albatross is built for life in the air. It flies vast distances—as much as 75,000 miles (120,000 km) in a year. Wandering albatrosses can live for 50 years and spend most of their lives at sea, only coming onto land to breed and raise their young. They dive into the sea to catch fish, squid, and octopus swimming close to the surface.

## Super flyers

When it comes to flying, wandering albatrosses are in a league of their own. They can fly at speeds of 45 mph (72 kph) and stay airborne for up to two days by catching the wind, making flapping unnecessary. By locking their wings in place, these birds can even fly when they're asleep.

## Pairs for life

Wandering albatrosses mate for life. Males attract females by spreading their wings, shaking their heads, and squawking. Once they have bonded as a couple, they raise a chick together every two years.

## Rocky nests

Wandering albatrosses nest on rocky cliffs and remote islands, building nests out of mud and grass. They have the longest incubation period of any bird, sitting on their eggs for up to 11 weeks. Once their chick is born, the parents take turns feeding and guarding it.

## Drinking seawater

Like many seabirds, wandering albatrosses can drink saltwater thanks to glands above the eyes that remove excess salt. When the glands are full, they excrete a salty snot that drains out through holes in the beak.

# Playtime

Young sea lions are as curious and playful as puppies. They use play to learn how to swim, hunt, and interact with other members of their social group. Sea lions are easy to tell apart from seals. They have small ears that stick out, and they can bend their hind flippers forward to support their weight and waddle around on land.

139

# Icy waters

At Earth's top and bottom are the coldest oceans. At the North Pole is the Arctic Ocean—an icy ocean encircled by land. At the South Pole is the opposite: an icy continent encircled by sea—the Southern Ocean. Both of these oceans are rich in food and marine life, but the animals that live in them have to be tough. They must withstand long, brutal winters when the sun never rises and the water is either bitterly cold or frozen solid.

**Area**
184,000 square miles
(476,000 sq km)

**Average depth**
3,234 ft (1,004 m)

**Frozen**
Almost all year round

# Beaufort Sea

## This southern stretch of the Arctic Ocean is covered in thick sheets of ice for most of the year.

Even in summer, the surface temperature of the Beaufort Sea, situated off the northern coasts of Alaska and Canada, remains at near freezing. Despite these chilly conditions, marine life thrives. This is because the sea's nutrient-rich waters nourish plankton—the foundation of many food chains in the sea.

### Life under ice

Ice plays a major role in the lives of animals in the Beaufort Sea. Some crustaceans live on its underside and hide from predators in cracks. Mammals such as whales and seals need to find or make holes in the ice to breathe air.

The ringed seal is one of four species of seals found in the Beaufort Sea.

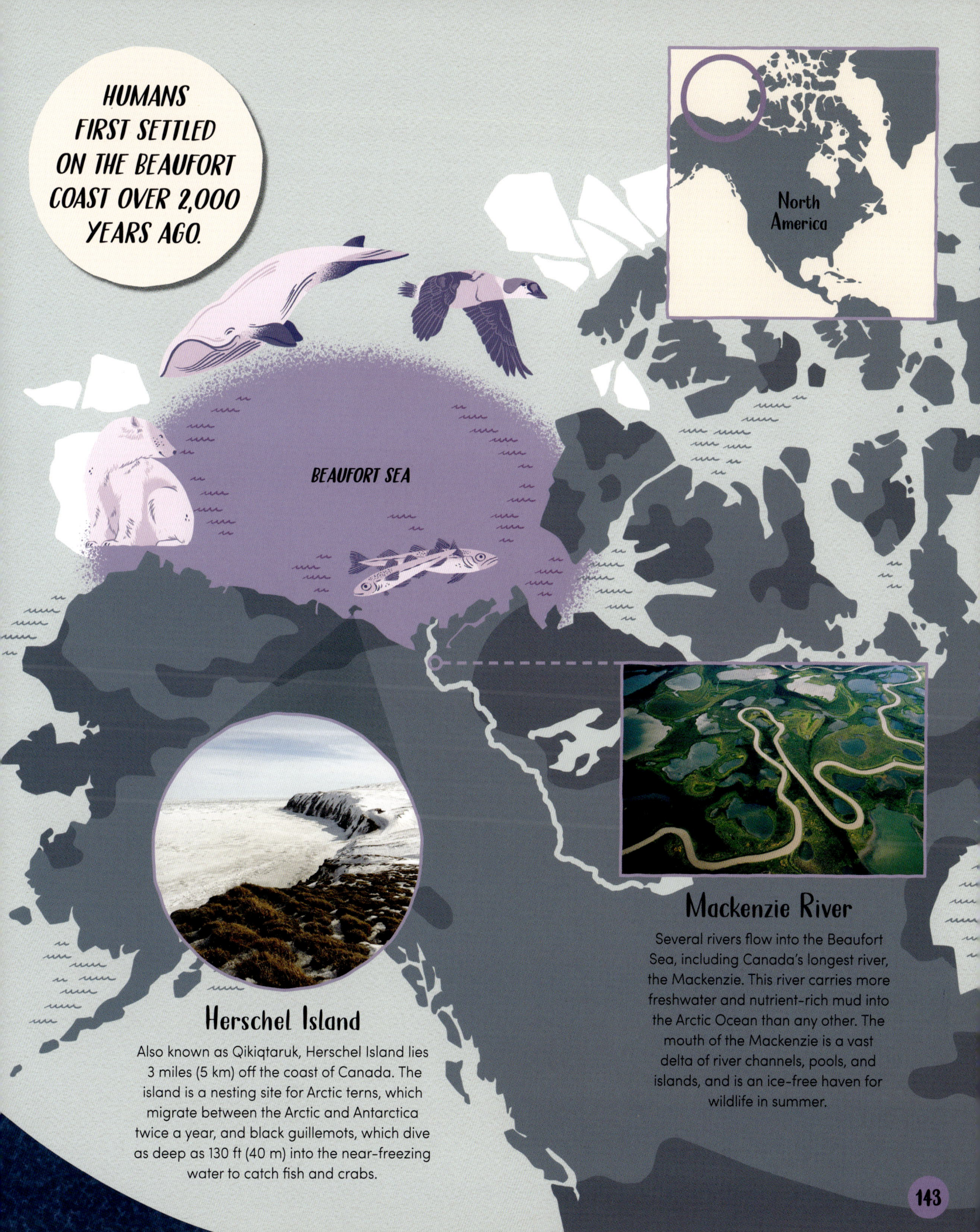

HUMANS FIRST SETTLED ON THE BEAUFORT COAST OVER 2,000 YEARS AGO.

North America

BEAUFORT SEA

## Herschel Island

Also known as Qikiqtaruk, Herschel Island lies 3 miles (5 km) off the coast of Canada. The island is a nesting site for Arctic terns, which migrate between the Arctic and Antarctica twice a year, and black guillemots, which dive as deep as 130 ft (40 m) into the near-freezing water to catch fish and crabs.

## Mackenzie River

Several rivers flow into the Beaufort Sea, including Canada's longest river, the Mackenzie. This river carries more freshwater and nutrient-rich mud into the Arctic Ocean than any other. The mouth of the Mackenzie is a vast delta of river channels, pools, and islands, and is an ice-free haven for wildlife in summer.

# Geography of the Beaufort Sea

The Beaufort Sea is a vast expanse of ocean that's about the same size as the state of California. The sea's frigid waters are among the least explored in the world. Its coastlines are made up of tundra, lagoons, tidal flats, and glaciers. Surviving in this icy world isn't easy, but many animals have adapted to life here.

## Arctic seasons

In summer, there is sunlight all day and all night over the Beaufort Sea. But winter is the opposite, with months of darkness illuminated only by the moon, stars, and amazing displays of the northern lights.

## Sea ice

The surface of the Beaufort Sea is frozen over for 10 months of the year, with the ice almost 6.5 ft (2 m) thick in some places. Many animals depend on the ice for survival. For example, polar bears hunt on it and seals nest on it. In summer, the sea ice breaks up and thaws near the coastline, as shown here.

## Beaufort Gyre

Swirling around the Beaufort Sea is a circular current known as the Beaufort Gyre. This massive, slow-moving whirlpool drags young, thin sea ice into its center, where it thickens. The amount of sea ice in the gyre has been decreasing in recent years as a result of climate change.

The wind blows the Beaufort Gyre in a clockwise direction.

The Transpolar Drift Stream is another major current in the Arctic Ocean, carrying water and ice from Siberia to Greenland.

Siberia

Greenland

Alaska

Canada

## Icebergs

When chunks of ice break off from the many glaciers along Alaska's and Canada's coastlines, they become icebergs. In Arctic waters, these floating chunks of ice range in size from around 16 ft (5 m) to several miles across. Only a fraction of an iceberg sits above the surface; most of it is hidden beneath the water.

## Bowhead whale
### (Balaena mysticetus)

This large whale is built for life under the ice. It has a huge head with a thick skull that it uses to break through the ice when it needs to breathe. The bowhead is thought to be the longest-living mammal, possibly reaching 200 years.

## Sea butterfly
### (Limacina helicina)

This tiny marine snail doesn't crawl across the seafloor—it flies through the water instead, using a pair of modified feet as wings. The sea butterfly eats plankton, which it catches in a net made of slime.

# Animals of the Beaufort Sea

Despite the icy cold conditions, the Beaufort Sea supports a bounty of life. Small crustaceans known as krill are the main food for many animals here, from seabirds to whales. In the bitter Arctic winter, when the sun disappears and the sea freezes over, some animals survive in the dark waters under the ice.

## King eider
### (Somateria spectabilis)

This large sea duck is a champion diver, capable of reaching depths of 180 ft (55 m), where it feeds on the shellfish, sea urchins, and starfish of the seafloor. The king eider nests inland, but its young move to the sea as soon as they can fly.

## Walrus
### *(Odobenus rosmarus)*

This large member of the seal family has distinctive tusks and a mustache of stiff whiskers. The tusks are special teeth that can grow to 3 ft (1 m) long. It uses them to help it clamber onto ice and to fight predators and other walruses. The whiskers are highly sensitive and help it find clams on the murky, dark seafloor.

## Arctic krill
### *(Thysanoessa raschii)*

Arctic krill are shrimplike crustaceans that gather in huge swarms, making them a vital food source for many Arctic species, including whales, seals, fish, and seabirds. They live to about three years and grow to 1 in (2.5 cm) in length.

## Snow crab
### *(Chionoecetes opilio)*

Snow crabs start life red but turn an olive color when they get older. They prey on smaller invertebrates and scavenge for food. To communicate with one another, snow crabs wave and drum their claws.

## Snow cave

There aren't many places to hide on the sea ice. That's why ringed seals build caves in the snow to give birth and nurse their newborns. The caves include a hole through the ice so the seals can come and go without being seen by polar bears.

Snow cave

Ringed seal with pup

Hole in ice

## Swimming

Polar bears are excellent swimmers. They use a dog-paddle style, propelling themselves with their forelegs and steering with their hind legs. One polar bear was recorded swimming 426 miles (687 km) over nine days in the Beaufort Sea, searching for seals on fragments of sea ice.

# Polar bear

An icon of the Arctic, the polar bear is the largest species of bear. Males, which are much larger than females, can reach 10 ft (3 m) in length and weigh up to 1,700 lb (770 kg). Polar bears spend most of their life on sea ice—patches of frozen seawater that float on the ocean's surface. In recent years, sea ice has been disappearing across the Arctic due to climate change, making life harder for the bears.

## Hunting

Unlike other bears, whose diets contain a mix of plants and animals, polar bears eat almost nothing but meat. Their favorite prey are seals, which they catch by sniffing out their dens hidden in the snow. If they can't find any dens, the bears will look for holes in the ice that the seals use to surface for air and ambush them there.

## Breeding

Female polar bears, known as sows, give birth to 1–3 cubs in winter, usually every three years. They dig deep dens in the snow on land or on sea ice before giving birth. The sows and their cubs hunker down in these cosy dens until spring.

Guard hair

Guard hairs are see-through with a hollow core. They scatter light in all directions, making polar bears white for camouflage on snow and ice.

Guard hairs

Underfur

Black skin

Fat layer

## Keeping warm

Polar bears can withstand temperatures as low as –50°F (–46°C) thanks to a thick fat layer and a two-layered fur coat. The first layer, known as underfur, consists of short, fuzzy hairs that trap heat close to the bear's skin, which is black. The second layer is made up of long, coarse guard hairs that repel water like a raincoat.

### Pod life

Beluga whales are highly social mammals that live in groups of up to 25 friends and family members. They communicate using many different sounds, including squeaks, chirps, whistles, and trills, as well as with facial expressions.

# Beluga whale

With its white body and squishy, bulbous head, the beluga whale is one of the most distinctive whales. This creature is known for its wide range of sounds, giving it the nickname "canary of the sea." Unlike other whales, the beluga has a flexible neck, so it can move its head up, down, and side to side, which helps it catch slippery prey on the seafloor.

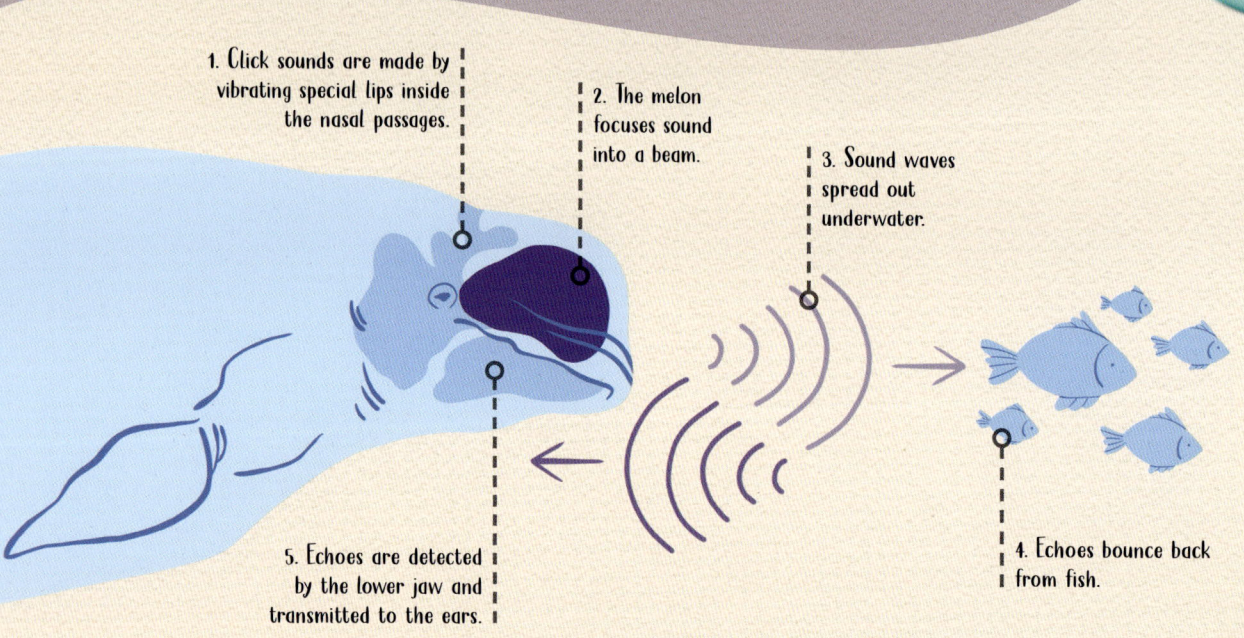

1. Click sounds are made by vibrating special lips inside the nasal passages.

2. The melon focuses sound into a beam.

3. Sound waves spread out underwater.

4. Echoes bounce back from fish.

5. Echoes are detected by the lower jaw and transmitted to the ears.

## Echolocation

When the water is dark or murky, belugas use sound to "see." They produce a series of clicklike noises that are focused into a beam of sound waves by an organ called a melon inside their bulbous forehead. The echoes that rebound from objects allow the whale to visualize them.

## Peg teeth

Beluga whales have around 36–40 peg-shaped teeth, which aren't particularly sharp. They aren't used for chewing but for holding onto small, slippery prey—including fish, squid, and worms—that belugas find on the seafloor and swallow whole.

## Arctic survivors

Beluga whales are perfectly adapted to life in the Arctic Ocean. Beneath their skin is a layer of fat around 5 in (13 cm) thick that insulates their body from the cold. They lack a dorsal fin on their back, allowing them to swim with ease under the ice. Their white skin camouflages belugas against floating ice, helping them hide from predatory orcas and polar bears.

# Whale pod

Bowhead whales normally live alone or in small pods (groups), but larger pods are sometimes seen at feeding sites. Bowheads are the only Arctic whales that are filter feeders. Instead of using teeth to catch fish, they use giant sieves in their mouths to strain shrimp from the water. This involves gulping huge volumes of seawater, which is why bowheads have the largest mouths of any animal.

# Glossary

### ADAPTATION
A change in an organism over time that enables it to become better suited to its habitat.

### ALGAE
Simple, plantlike organisms that live in water and make their food by photosynthesis.

### ANTARCTIC
Region around the South Pole.

### AQUATIC
A term used to describe organisms that live in water.

### ARCTIC
Region around the North Pole.

### ATMOSPHERE
The layer of air that surrounds Earth, held in place by gravity.

### ATOLL
A ring-shaped coral island or a ring-shaped group of coral islands surrounding a lagoon.

### BACTERIA
Microscopic single-celled organisms that make up one of the main kingdoms of life on Earth. Many bacteria are helpful but some cause diseases.

### BIOLUMINESCENCE
Production of light by a living organism.

### BLOWHOLE
A hole or pair of holes on the top of a whale's or dolphin's head, through which it breathes air.

### BLUBBER
Thick layer of fat that protects a marine mammal from the cold.

### CAMOUFLAGED
Colored, patterned, or shaped to match the surroundings. Animals use camouflage to hide.

### CANYON
Steep-sided valley in the seabed.

### CARBON DIOXIDE
A gas found in air. Animals breathe out carbon dioxide as a waste product, but plants absorb it.

### CELL
A tiny unit of living matter. Cells are the building blocks of all living things.

### CLIMATE
Weather that is typical for a specific area over a long period of time.

### CLIMATE CHANGE
Long-term changes in temperature and weather across Earth.

### COLONY
Large group of one species of animals or plants, whose members all live close together.

### CONTINENT
One of the seven large landmasses on Earth, mainly surrounded by sea.

### CONTINENTAL SHELF
The submerged edge of a continent that lies beneath shallow coastal seas.

### CONTINENTAL SLOPE
The edge of a continental shelf, which tilts down to the ocean floor.

### CORAL
A small marine animal that catches food with stinging tentacles. Coral reefs form from the hard skeletons of corals that live in large colonies.

### CORAL REEF
Rocklike structure formed by groups of corals in the warm waters along tropical coasts. Many fish and other sea creatures live around coral reefs.

### CRUST
The cool, rocky outer shell of Earth.

### CRUSTACEAN
An invertebrate with a hard exoskeleton, gills, and usually more than 10 pairs of limbs, such as a shrimp or lobster. Most crustaceans live in water.

### CURRENT
The movement of water in a specific direction.

### DELTA
An area of land formed from sediment deposited where a river meets the sea.

### DORSAL FIN
The single fin on the back of an animal such as a dolphin.

### ECHOLOCATION
A way of sensing objects by producing sound and listening for echoes. Beluga whales and dolphins use echolocation to "see" in dark or in murky water.

### ECOSYSTEM
A community of living things and their environment. An ecosystem may be as small as a pond or as large as a rainforest.

### ENVIRONMENT
The living and nonliving surroundings in which an animal lives, including land and weather.

### EQUATOR
An imaginary circle around the center of Earth, dividing it into the Northern and Southern Hemispheres (halves).

### EROSION
The wearing away of rock by natural forces, such as flowing water, wind, or glaciers.

### ESTUARY
A partially enclosed body of water where freshwater from a river meets the sea.

### EVAPORATION
A process by which a liquid changes into a gas.

### FJORD
A former glacial valley on the coast that has become an inlet of the sea.

### FRESHWATER
Water that is not salty, such as rivers and ponds.

## GILL
An organ used to breathe underwater.

## GLOBAL WARMING
The rise in the Earth's average temperature.

## HABITAT
Natural home of plants or animals, such as a seagrass meadow or coral reef.

## ICEBERG
Part of a glacier or ice shelf that has broken off and floated out to sea.

## INVERTEBRATE
Animal without a backbone.

## KRILL
Small crustacean of the open seas that is eaten by many larger ocean animals.

## LAGOON
An area of sheltered, shallow sea water, almost cut off from the open ocean.

## LARVA
The early stage in the life cycle of an animal that undergoes a major change when it develops into an adult.

## LATITUDE
A measure of how far north or south from the equator a location is. The equator has a latitude of 0°. The North Pole has a latitude of 90°.

## LIFE CYCLE
The changes a living thing goes through over its lifetime.

## MAMMAL
A warm-blooded vertebrate animal that feeds milk to its young.

## MANGROVE
A type of tree that grows on tropical coasts and has stiltlike roots to stay above the water.

## MARINE
A term that describes organisms that live in the sea.

## METHANE
A natural gas that burns easily and is used as fuel. It is a greenhouse gas.

## MICROORGANISM
An organism too small to be seen with the naked eye, such as a bacterium.

## MIDOCEAN RIDGE
A submarine mountain chain created by volcanoes erupting from a rift in the ocean floor.

## MIGRATION
Movement of animals or people from one place to another. Usually seasonal and for protection, feeding, or breeding.

## NOCTURNAL
Active at night but inactive during the day.

## NUTRIENTS
Substances that animals and plants take in and that are essential for life and growth.

## ORGAN
A specialized part of an animal or plant that carries out a particular task, such as a stomach or a brain.

## ORGANISM
A living thing.

## OXYGEN
A gas in the air that all living things need to live.

## PARASITE
An organism that lives on or inside another organism (a host) and gets its food from (or at the expense of) the host. Parasites are often harmful to the host.

## PHOTOSYNTHESIS
The process by which plants use the sun's energy to make food molecules from water and carbon dioxide.

## PHYTOPLANKTON
The tiny, mostly single-celled organisms that live in the surface waters of oceans and lakes and are the base of most aquatic food chains.

## PLANKTON
Organisms that float in water and drift with the currents. Most plankton are small.

## POLYP
A form taken by some marine animals, such as jellyfish, sea anemones, and corals. Polyps have a mouth at one end, and are attached firmly at the base to a rock or the seabed.

## PREDATOR
An animal that hunts and eats other animals.

## PREY
An animal hunted by other animals for food.

## SCHOOL
A large group of fish that swim together in the same direction and in a coordinated style.

## SEAMOUNT
An underwater volcano on the ocean floor that is fully submerged.

## SEDIMENT
Small fragments of rock, sand, or mud that settle in layers, usually underwater.

## SPECIES
A particular type of organism, such as a tiger shark or a manatee. Members of the same species can breed together.

## STREAMLINED
Smoothly shaped to move easily through water.

## TENTACLE
A long, boneless, flexible body part that underwater animals, such as squids and octopuses, use for touching or holding.

## TIDE
The regular rise and fall of the ocean, caused by forces from the sun and the moon.

## TRENCH
A steep-sided trough or valley in the ocean floor.

## TROPICS
The regions of Earth close to the equator, where the climate is warm all year round.

## WATER VAPOR
An invisible gas formed when water evaporates into the air.

## ZOOPLANKTON
Tiny animals and larvae (immature animals) that live as plankton in the sea surface.

# Index

# Acknowledgments

DK would like to thank the following people for their help in creating this book: Emma Clayton for design assistance; Katie John for proofreading; Stephen Johnson for image retouching; Vijay Kandwal and Syed Md Farhan for DTP assistance; Manpreet Kaur for picture credits assistance; Helen Peters for indexing; Jacqui Swan for picture research assistance.

The publisher would like to thank the following for their kind permission to reproduce their photographs:

(Key: a-above; b-below/bottom; c-centre; f-far; l-left; r-right; t-top)

1-160 Dreamstime.com: Jackreznor (Background). 4-5 Getty Images: Mike Hill. 6-7 BluePlanetArchive.com: Doug Perrine. 8-9 Getty Images: Matteo Colombo. 10-11 Alamy Stock Photo: Alex Mustard / Nature Picture Library. 12-13 Alamy Stock Photo: Josh Anon / Jaynes Gallery / DanitaDelimont.com. 14-15 Alamy Stock Photo: Doug Allan / Bluegreen Pictures. 16 Alamy Stock Photo: Eric Gevaert (tr). 17 Alamy Stock Photo: SeaTops (cr); WaterFrame_dpr (br). Dreamstime.com: Dudlajzov (tl); Seadam (cra). 20 Alamy Stock Photo: Nature Picture Library / Jurgen Freund (ca/Squid). Getty Images: Moment / Humberto Ramirez (c); Photodisc / Roland Birke (cb/Zooplankton). naturepl.com: Doug Perrine (ca). Science Photo Library: Marek Mis (cb). 21 Alamy Stock Photo: Nature Picture Library / Pascal Kobeh (ca); Nature Picture Library / Georgette Douwma (cra). Getty Images: Moment / A. Martin UW Photography (c). naturepl.com: Andy Murch (cr). Science Photo Library: Pacific Ring Of Fire 2004 Expedition. NOAA Office Of Ocean Exploration; Dr. Bob Embley, NOAA Pmel, Chief Scientist (br). 22-23 Dreamstime.com: Paul Topp (b). 23 Getty Images: Moment / by Andrea Pucci (cra); Moment / Joe Daniel Price (cr). 24 Alamy Stock Photo: Planetpix (cr). Getty Images / iStock: richcarey (tl). Getty Images: Alexis Rosenfeld (br). 25 Alamy Stock Photo: NOAA (br). Getty Images / iStock: E+ / AscentXmedia (tr). NOAA: News April 30 2014 (tl). 26-27 naturepl.com: Alex Mustard. 28 Alamy Stock Photo: Stocktrek Images, Inc. (tr). Getty Images / iStock: Aaron Bull (bl). 30 Getty Images / iStock: vojce (bl). 30-31 naturepl.com: Juergen Freund (b). 31 Science Photo Library: Frank Fox (br). Shutterstock.com: marcobrivio.photography (tr). 32 123RF.com: whitcomberd (cla, bl). Dreamstime.com: Gary Hanna / Pardentevamaya (crb); Shane Myers (tr). 33 Alamy Stock Photo: Brandon Cole Marine Photography (cl); Fred Bavendam / Minden Pictures (tl); Jeff Mondragon (bl); lophius_sub (br). Dreamstime.com: Apidech Ninkhlai / Joeyphoto (cra). 34-35 Alamy Stock Photo: Nature Picture Library / Alex Mustard. 34 Dreamstime.com: TUNATURA (bc). 35 Science Photo Library: Scubazoo (crb). 36 Dreamstime.com: Puntasit Choksawatdikorn (tl); Whitcomberd (br). 36-37 Alamy Stock Photo: mauritius images GmbH / Reinhard Dirscherl (t). 37 Alamy Stock Photo: Juergen Freund (br). 38-39 Alamy Stock Photo: van der Meer Marica / Arterra Picture Library. 41 Alamy Stock Photo: Danita Delimont / Jaynes Gallery (tr); Images & Stories (tc). 42 Dreamstime.com: Seadam (cl). 42-43 Getty Images: Moment / Matteo Colombo (t). 43 Getty Images / iStock: E+ / Richmatts (cr). 44 123RF.com: cookelma (bl). Alamy Stock Photo: Reinhard Dirscherl (tl). 44-45 Alamy Stock Photo: Nature Picture Library / Linda Pitkin (bc); WaterFrame_dpr (tc). 45 Alamy Stock Photo: Genevieve Vallee (cl). naturepl.com: Georgette Douwma (tr). Shutterstock.com: Amirkhans world (br). 46 Alamy Stock Photo: Cyrille Mulard / Biosphoto (tl); Pete Oxford / Minden Pictures (br); Nature Picture Library / Sue Daly (cra). 47 Alamy Stock Photo: Avalon. red / Oceans Image (cla); Zoonar / Erich Teister - etfoto (tr); ImageArt (br). naturepl.com: Alex Mustard (cl). 48-49 Getty Images: Moment / Colors and shapes of underwater world. 49 Alamy Stock Photo: WaterFrame_fur (clb). Science Photo Library: Ted Kinsman (tr). 50-51 naturepl.com: Klein & Hubert. 52-53 Getty Images: Moment / Douglas Klug. 55 Alamy Stock Photo: Antonio Busiello (bl). 56 Alamy Stock Photo: Greg Vaughn (bl). Getty Images: Moment / Matt Mawson (crb). 56-57 Getty Images: Moment / Douglas Klug. 58 Alamy Stock Photo: F1online digitale Bildagentur GmbH / Tobias Friedrich (tl). Dreamstime.com: Derek Holzapfel (crb). 58-59 BluePlanetArchive.com: David Wrobel (ca). 59 Alamy Stock Photo: mauritius images GmbH / Gabi Reichert (clb). Dreamstime.com: Derek Holzapfel (tr); Kelpfish (crb). 60 Dreamstime.com: Aliaksandr Karpovich. 61 Dreamstime.com: Jeanninebryan (clb). Getty Images: Valerie Rondone / 500px (tr); Moment / Alan Vernon (cla). naturepl.com: Ralph Pace (br). 62 Alamy Stock Photo: Jean-Philippe Delobelle / Biosphoto (cr); Blue Planet Archive (l). 62-63 Alamy Stock Photo: BIOSPHOTO / Bruno Guenard (bc). 63 Alamy Stock Photo: Blue Planet Archive (tl, cl); Nature Picture Library / Nick Upton (tr). 64-65 Alamy Stock Photo: Alex Mustard / Nature Picture Library. 66 naturepl.com: Shane Gross (tl); Doug Perrine (bc). 68 Getty Images: DigitalVision / Abstract Aerial Art (br). naturepl.com: Shane Gross (bl). 68-69 Getty Images: DigitalVision / Abstract Aerial Art (t). 70 Alamy Stock Photo: SeaTops (bl). Getty Images / iStock: E+ / hocus-focus (tl). naturepl.com: Pascal Kobeh (tr). 71 naturepl.com: Alex Mustard (bl); Gary Bell / Oceanwide (cla); Tui De Roy (tr). 72 Alamy Stock Photo: Brent Barnes / Stocktrek Images (bl). 72-73 Getty Images: Moment Open / by wildestanimal (b). 73 Ardea: Paulo Di Oliviera (cra). BluePlanetArchive.com: Eric Cheng (tl). 74 Alamy Stock Photo: Nature Picture Library / Jurgen Freund (bl). Rachel Austin: (tr). 75 Alamy Stock Photo: imageBROKER / Mathieu Foulquie (cl); Suzanne Long (tr). 76-77 Getty Images: photography by Maico Presente. 78-79 Getty Images: Moment / Taken by Andrew Thirlwell. 81 naturepl.com: Shane Gross (crb). 82 Getty Images: Olivier Morin / AFP. 83 Dreamstime.com: Tsvibrav (br). naturepl.com: Doug Perrine (cl). 84 Alamy Stock Photo: imageBROKER / Rolf von Riedmatten (tl); Nature Picture Library / Jurgen Freund (bl); Stephen Frink Collection (br). 85 Alamy Stock Photo: Michael Greenfelder (cla); WaterFrame_mus (tr, cra); Doug Perrine (br). 86 Alamy Stock Photo: imageBROKER / Rolf von Riedmatten. 87 Alamy Stock Photo: Pat Bennett (clb); Natural Visions / Heather Angel (br). naturepl.com: Solvin Zankl (bl). 88 Alamy Stock Photo: Science Photo Library / Steve Gschmeissner (tl). Science Photo Library: Wim Van Egmond (bl, tr). 89 BluePlanetArchive.com: Steven Kovacs (cra). Science Photo Library: John Clegg (bl); Steve Gschmeissner (tl). 90-91 naturepl.com: Shane Gross. **93 Alamy Stock Photo:** Xinhua (cl). © **Caladan Oceanic:** Esri (br). **94 NOAA:** Office of Ocean Exploration and Research, 2016 Deepwater Exploration of the Marianas. (t). **95 NOAA:** Office of Ocean Exploration and Research, 2016 Deepwater Exploration of the Marianas (bl). **Science Photo Library:** JAN HINSCH (crb). **96 NOAA:** Office of Ocean Exploration and Research, 2016 Deepwater Exploration of the Marianas (bl); Okeanos Explorer Program, 2016 Deepwater Exploration of the Marianas, Leg 1 (br). **97 NOAA:** Office of Ocean Exploration and Research, 2016 Deepwater Exploration of the Marianas. (cra). **Ocean Networks Canada:** (t). **Science Photo Library:** Dante Fenolio (b). **98 Getty Images / iStock:** 3dsam79 (tr). **99 Alamy Stock Photo:** David DesRochers (bl); Adisha Pramod (br). **naturepl.com:** Solvin Zankl (cra, crb). **100-101 naturepl.com:** Solvin Zankl. **103 Alamy Stock Photo:** Universal Images Group North America LLC / Planet Observer (tr). **Science Photo Library:** Kaj R. Svensson (cla). **104 NASA:** OB.DAAC (t). **104-105 NASA:** GSFC / MODIS Rapid Response (bc). **105 Ocean Exploration Trust:** (t). **Science Photo Library:** I Macdonald / OAR / National Undersea Research Program / Texas A&M University / NOAA (br). **106 Alamy Stock Photo:** Helmut Corneli (tr); Richard Herrmann / Minden Pictures (cla). **Getty Images / iStock:** johnandersonphoto (bl). **106-107 Alamy Stock Photo:** WaterFrame_fur (b). **107 Alamy Stock Photo:** Lee Dalton (c); Nature Picture Library / Alex Mustard (clb). **naturepl.com:** Franco Banfi (t); Solvin Zankl (crb). **Science Photo Library:** Dante Fenolio (br). **108 Alamy Stock Photo:** Pat Bonish (bl); imageBROKER / Mathieu Foulquie (tr). **108-109 Getty Images:** Moment / James R.D. Scott. **109 Alamy Stock Photo:** Michele and Tom Grimm (cra). **110 Getty Images:** Moment / Beachmite Photography (c). **naturepl.com:** Tui De Roy (bl). **110-111 naturepl.com:** Shane P. White. **111 Getty Images:** Moment / Samuel J Coe. **112-113 Alamy Stock Photo:** Rodrigo Friscione / Connect Images. **114-115 Getty Images:** Posnov. **117 naturepl.com:** David Hall (b). **118 NASA:** Jesse Allen, Earth Observatory, using data obtained from the University of Marylands Global Land Cover Facility. (t). **119 Getty Images:** Moment / somnuk krokbum (b). **120 Alamy Stock Photo:** Mark Smith (cla); Pradeep Soman (tr); Rob Walls (b). **121 Alamy Stock Photo:** Brian Bevan (br); imageBROKER / F. Schneider (bl). **Dreamstime.com:** Chirasak Tolertmongkol (cl). **122 Dreamstime.com:** Oliver Carsten Sommer (tr). **naturepl.com:** Pedro Narra (tr). **122-123 naturepl.com:** Ripan Biswas (b). **123 Alamy Stock Photo:** Jason Edwards (tc). **124 Dreamstime.com:** Snion19 (br). **Getty Images:** somnuk krokbum (l). **Science Photo Library:** Jim Edds (tr). **125 Alamy Stock Photo:** Jurgen Freund / Nature Picture Library (cl); Chris Mattison (tl). **Dreamstime.com:** Rattanakorn Songrenoo (br). **Science Photo Library:** Thierry Berrod, Mona Lisa Production (tr). **126-127 naturepl.com:** Shane Gross. **129 Alamy Stock Photo:** LWM / NASA / LANDSAT (br). **Dreamstime.com:** Max Maximov Photography (cl). **130-131 Alamy Stock Photo:** imageBROKER / Sascha Selli-Grabowski. **Getty Images:** Fotografías Jorge León Cabello (tc). **131 Getty Images / iStock:** Brockswood (cr). **132 Alamy Stock Photo:** Arco / G. Lacz / Imagebroker (bl); Kevin Schafer / Minden Pictures (tr). **Getty Images:** by wildestanimal (tl). **133 Alamy Stock Photo:** SeaTops (c). **Getty Images / iStock:** Grafissimo (t). **134-135 Alamy Stock Photo:** Wayne Lynch / All Canada Photos. **135 Alamy Stock Photo:** David Osborn (bc); Yva Momatiuk & John Eastcott / Minden Pictures (ca). **Getty Images:** Paul Souders (cr). **136-137 Alamy Stock Photo:** Suzi Eszterhas / Minden Pictures. **136 Alamy Stock Photo:** Andy Rouse / Avalon.red (br). **137 Alamy Stock Photo:** Chris & Monique Fallows / Nature Picture Library (clb). **naturepl.com:** TJ Rich (br). **138-139 Getty Images:** by wildestanimal. **140-141 naturepl.com:** Paul Souders / Worldfoto. **143 Alamy Stock Photo:** J.A. Kraulis / All Canada Photos (crb). **Shutterstock.com:** Wirestock Creators (cb). **144 Alamy Stock Photo:** Hugh Rose / DanitaDelimont (tr). **144-145 Dreamstime.com:** Karen Foley (b). **145 Getty Images:** Keith Calandro / 500px (c). **146 Alamy Stock Photo:** Staffan Widstrand / Nature Picture Library (bl); Flip Nicklin / Minden Pictures (tl). **Science Photo Library:** Alexander Semenov (cr). **147 BluePlanetArchive:** Amar & Isabelle Guillen (bl). **Russell R Hopcroft:** (tl). **naturepl.com:** Steven Kazlowski (tr). **148 Alamy Stock Photo:** imageBROKER.com GmbH & Co. KG / E. Baccega (br); Jose B. Ruiz / Nature Picture Library (tl); Gabrielle & Michel Therin-Weise / robertharding (cra). **149 naturepl.com:** Danny Green. **150-151 Alamy Stock Photo:** WorldFoto (b). **naturepl.com:** Doc White (t). **151 BluePlanetArchive.com:** Wyland (tc). **152-153 naturepl.com:** Tony Wu.

**Cover images: Front and Back: Dreamstime.com:** Altitudevs b, Seadam c; **Getty Images / iStock:** E+ / cinoby cb; **Front: Alamy Stock Photo:** Gustavo Adolfo Rojas Segovia br; **Dreamstime.com:** Daniel Poloha bl; **Getty Images:** Moment / WraithHao t; **Back: Alamy Stock Photo:** Gustavo Adolfo Rojas Segovia bl; **Getty Images:** Moment / WraithHao t